OPERA

OPERA

BY

RICHARD CAPELL

ERNEST BENN LIMITED
LONDON

DEDICATED TO

PILCHER WRIGHTSON ESQ.

First published - 1930
Second Revised Edition - 1948

PUBLISHED BY ERNEST BENN LIMITED
BOUVERIE HOUSE, FLEET STREET, LONDON
PRINTED IN THE NETHERLANDS
BY HOLDERT & CO. N.V., AMSTERDAM

CONTENTS

I

THE NATURE OF OPERA

THE drama of antiquity and of the middle ages is known to have made use of music, although we do not know precisely to what effect. The constituents of opera all have remote origins. Opera itself, however, is a creation of modern times. In olden days music was ancillary: beautiful, effective and highly considered, no doubt, but still no more than the accompaniment of liturgies, festivities, dancing and recitation. Modern musicians — that is, from the Renaissance onwards — have created a more elaborate, eloquent and self-reliant art. The great instrumental forms present, indeed, a music that is considerable purely for music's sake.

Music is primarily song. It is probable that the significance of instrumental music rests mainly on an analogy which the listener more or less consciously draws between any sound he hears and vocal utterance. Opera is song at its greatest forcefulness, in its greatest variety. For all the increase in the resources of music — so much more abundant and complex than anything the ancient world dreamt of — the old reason has held good for the association of music and drama: namely, the power of music to magnify the verbal expression of emotion. Music and the word are indissociable. Only the old relation of servant and master has been changed into a partnership in which music maintains (if in varying degrees) predominance. In the predominance of music — in the essentially musical importance of a work in which music is supported by other factors — lies the nature of opera. And just as Greek drama — its theatre, its actors, its music lost — still leaves behind a residue of pure poetry, so would opera — its theatre lost, its actors, its play — still leave pure music, the Leonora overtures, "Ocean, thou mighty monster!", the preludes to *Lohengrin* and *Tristan.*

We cannot, without affectation or freakishness, sing without words. The variety and the forms of words are part of the music of song. As for the meaning of words, this may in one instance be an incidental resource of which the musician takes more or less advantage; or in another it may be the prime agent, the inspiration of a composer's musical thought and the channel connecting him with the world of general human experience. Words are links with the particularities of life. There is a music that is engendered by music alone, but it tends to become over-formalized and academic. The artist takes in cognizance of life through every aperture of the mind; the experiences of all the senses contribute to the making of great music.

Opera then is, in the most technical aspect, the great field for the intensive cultivation of vocal music — the field for the singer's most powerful, passionate and expansive efforts. As an inspiration, it affords, from the sources of dramatic language and the visual impressions of the scene, suggestions that have incited musicians to a long and brilliant succession of inventions in accent, colour and form. Even the introversive composer, though he may not be practically interested, cannot but be indirectly influenced. The extraversive finds here incomparable opportunities of contact and creates in opera, if not the most sublime works of his art, at least those in which the visible and tangible sides of life are represented with the clearest definition and the greatest vividness and variety.

Opera* was a late flower of the secularization of the arts which followed upon the Revival

* i.e., *opera musicale*. Cavalli's *Teti* (Venice, 1639) was the first opera so called. Previous operas had been called *favola in musica, dramma musicale,* and so on.

of Learning and the recession of the authority of the medieval Church. It was the age of a new individualism. A cosmology had broken down. A new importance was felt in the expression of personal experiences. Drama was revived and dramatic song was invented. In the thirteenth century such particular utterances would have seemed trivial; but now the centre of things had shifted and each soul was its own universe. Orpheus and Ariadne expressed passions, not beliefs; were assertive, not repressed. This spelt a new realism. The middle ages may be thought of as surviving in music well through the Renaissance and flowering their last in sixteenth-century polyphony. Palestrina died in 1594. This was the year of the first opera, Jacopo Peri's *Dafne.* Thereafter music, which had been predominantly liturgical, has been predominantly personal and dramatic.

To-day there may seem nothing in the music of Peri and the Florentine camerata to explain the exciting success it enjoyed. One thing to be remembered is that Peri the shock-headed ("zazzerino") was a brilliant actor-singer whose gaunt recitative was a vehicle for his thrilling declamatory gift. Such things have often to be remembered in the course of a survey, not simply of the noblest, most durable music opera

has produced, but of opera in general. A word
has been given to the stimulating encounters
music may make in the theatre. The contacts are,
however, varied, the company mixed. The theatre is the world, its life is that of all men. Composers of opera have commonly been faced with
more than they knew how to grapple with; and
so with the critic of opera, who is enslaving himself to a kind of scholastic realism — to the
superstition of the virtue of a word — if, because opera is called a form of artistic activity,
as are the sonnet and fugue, he attempts to lay
down for opera anything like the rules of fugue
or of the sonnet, which are vessels for the dis-
tilled thought of the solitary mind. Opera is
more like architecture or the novel in its diversity of modes, and in that it has entertained not
a few, but a vast diversity of men, the high and
the low, of South and North; playing a social
part and adapting itself in the course of centuries
to this or that regimen or constitution. It would
be possible to compose a social history of the
Europe of the last 300 years in terms of opera,
and perhaps easier than to treat of operatic
music as a pure aesthetic concept.

Opera is justifiable by no beautiful theory;
but it exists, it interests; and therein and in the
sometimes incomparable fruit of its luxuriance

is its justification. To the cloistered mind, the field of opera presents a dishevelled and frantic look. Opera is worldly; it is a diversion, and diversion spells dissipation to one reader of life, while to another it is the prime opportunity. Opera is sociable; it means frivolity and waste to those who seek the eternal verities by elimination, but a wealth of knowledge to such as take the empirical way. And that way has not missed all the verities which has led to the serene groves of *Die Zauberflöte,* to Leonora's heroism, to the sublimation of passion in *Tristan* and of pessimism in *Götterdämmerung.* Without opera modern music is hardly conceivable. It is the source of much of our instrumental music. The slow movement of the classical sonata and symphony grew out of the operatic *aria cantabile.* Sacred works like Mozart's and Verdi's Requiems and Beethoven's Masses derive more from opera than from liturgical traditions.* Beethoven's Mass in D may be called his principal dramatic composition. Characteristic, terse themes in his symphonies and quartets brought into pure music expressions of the conciseness of speech; and this is to be recognized as a derivation from

* In Bach the fugue and choral hymn are ecclesiastical, the recitatives and arias in the Passion and Cantataş operatic, in origin.

opera. The developments of instrumental music, on the other hand, have had their repercussions on the music of the theatre; Beethoven's symphonic style engendered Wagner's dramatic style with its rich ramifications and masterly transitions.

The composer of opera is a musician who is also possessed of the dramatist's instincts, though not necessarily possessing literary technics. The condition is very exigent; equilibrium is precarious, subject as it is to all manner of cross-influences. Thus there is no tradition of validity for the composition of opera; every generation and, latterly, almost every composer has had to cast a new type under the stress of the forces — drama, theatre, and all the currents of men's ever-changing thoughts — which are let loose upon music through the fateful association in the human voice of word and song. The composer who is rather more of a playwright than a musician (for example, Boito) is likely to fall short of the goal — the enduring achievement — no less than the musician who loses grip of drama in an absorbing exercise of his art. The former case is the rarer. The way of opera has been littered with the ephemeral works of those musicians who, while attracted by the theatre, have failed in the playwright's sense.

The magic of music is such that many of their works have at least enjoyed their day. If most operas have been failures in the view of posterity, many have well served their generation; and if a general principle is to be found underlying this service it is, perhaps, that opera as a form has practically appropriated to itself all poetry in the theatre, leaving to modern drama only prosaic expression.

The composer of opera clearly must have a theatre in view; his best opportunity will obviously be where the theatre is dignified and considered, a centre of the life of the community. The position of the edifice is symbolical in Vienna, in Paris, in the Italian and German cities. The great continental opera-houses speak of long and splendid musical traditions, as of cultivated aristocracies and of patriotic and civic pride. If the whole of music is not there, it is certainly not a coincidence that those monuments are most conspicuous, magnificent and time-honoured in the countries which have been most fertile in musical invention and have in the last 300 years given to the world the music it esteems the most.

The very thought of music as a gift to the world brings us against one of those paradoxes of opera which would of themselves make a chapter. (The most commonly alleged paradox is trivial, belonging as it does to the objections that would include the lack of a third dimension in pictorial representation. When there is anything in the contention that it is far-fetched or unnatural to sing such and such a dramatic utterance, there is a fault in the musician's choice of text or his treatment.) But it a serious paradox that music which, notwithstanding all its various dialects, is a general European language, should, when it comes to opera — the most readily and widely popular of its higher forms — find itself hedged about as it is not in fugue and Mass, symphony and quartet — namely, by the limitations of the curse of Babel.

The opera of the universal genius, as also that of purely popular scope, is a foreign thing once it has crossed a frontier, requiring adaptation (translation) if it is to be more than half understood, and even when most happily adapted still calling for a rarer sympathy and more cultivated curiosity than it ever needed at home. And with this limitation of opera there also goes that of time. If opera shows with a peculiar brilliance compared with the secluded forms of music, it is also peculiarly subject, thanks to its close relations with transient literary forms and fashions and to its dependence on certain social conditions, to superannuation and eclipse, from which works of supremely fine music even are not safe (for instance, Handel's forty-six operas).

There is another thing. The great opera-houses which suggest such possibilities of musical pleasure may also strike us as rather alarmingly official in look, and uncomfortably like temples, where faith is congealed in formulas. The huge establishment needed for the presentation of opera tends indeed to hinder easy evolution; and the history of opera shows us periods of over-formalization, and then the arrival of the reformer — Gluck, Wagner, Mussorgsky — who makes for a new contact with reality. Admirable music has often been written for the theatre by men who had not the dramatic impulse; but opera was created and has again and again been re-vivified by those who, while naturally expressing themselves in music, have principally desired to interpret life and address the world by the incomparably vivid means of a dramatic form.

The proper maintenance of opera is an extremely serious question. The establishment of this elaborate and splendid form of art was almost everywhere the care of autocrats and paternal governments whose courts it embellished and whose peoples it impressed and entertained.

The history of opera is principally Italian, French, German and, later, Russian. Opera flourished under the Italian tyrants of the baroque period, under Bourbons, Hapsburgs; at a score of German courts; under Romanovs. The political independence of the English people, in comparison with the Continent, afforded less facility for any such provision of official entertainment, while at the same time the taste of our royal house did not incline, at the favourable moment, to found a court theatre. The consequence is that opera has been with us principally a foreign importation.

The lack of a national opera has meant an inestimable impoverishment of our musical life. In Europe the democracies have simply continued to maintain the operatic institutions founded by their aristocratic predecessors. If we, in England, ever get opera soundly established it can only be by a democratic movement in favour of superior music such as history has not yet recorded.

In the United States of America the position is not unlike ours, except that the importations of opera are more lavish and the native creation less considerable.

II

THE ARCHAIC PERIOD

IT IS convenient to assign the beginnings of opera to a group of ingenious Florentines who in the closing years of the sixteenth century set themselves the task of recreating classic Greek tragedy, and to consider the lost *Dafne* (1595), by Jacopo Peri (1561-1633), as the first opera. The Florentine enterprise marked a turning point.

No artistic innovation arrives entirely unannounced. The authors of the first operas were not wholly original. While hardly anything was known in fact of the archaic music which they sought by intuition to revive, they had something to go upon in the musical and dramatic entertainments that had flourished at the Italian Courts since the beginnings of the Renaissance. These entertainments had in their turn derived from the Miracle Plays of the medieval Church which in the rich and exuberant Italy of the fifteenth century became remarkably splendid, as also from the pageants with which the great cities celebrated their patronal feasts and wel-

comed visiting princes and popes. This pageantry drew indifferently from sacred and pro-
fane lore. Thus Perugia in 1444 performed in
honour of Pope Eugenius IV. the story of the
Minotaur, the tragedy of Iphigenia, the Nat-
ivity and the Ascension.

At Florence in the fifteenth century the Miracle Play developed in the hands of the wealthy
confraternities of laymen into a well-defined
form, the *Sacra Rappresentazione,* to which the
most eminent poets, musicians and scenic engin-
eers contributed.*

Between the scenes madrigals and solo songs
were sung, and these interludes developed on
their own account, sometimes introducing pagan
idylls into Christian story.** According to
Vincenzo Borghini, the Florentine Miracle
Plays were, down to the beginning of the sixteenth century, wholly sung. The effect, like that
of the civic pageants with their processions,
dancing, tableaux-vivants and apotheosis, must
have had much of what we should call an oper-

* Lorenzo de' Medici himself wrote one of these
sacred dramas, forty-three of which were reprinted by
A. d'Ancona in 1872.
** In *Santa Uliva,* which lasted in all two days, the
fable of Narcissus and Echo was presented, and also
a masque of Night and the God of Sleep. (Symonds.)

atic character. Out of the English Miracle Plays came Elizabethan drama. The *Sacra Rappresentazione* turned out differently. Italy was not to have a national theatre in the French or English sense; but elements of the Florentine Representations have come down in the Italian form of a national theatre — namely, the opera.

One of the earliest plays written in Italian was the *Orfeo* of the scholar and poet Poliziano, which was produced at Mantua in 1472. This was a dramatic poem written on the lines of a Florentine Miracle Play, but on a pagan instead of a Christian fable. It was undoubtedly meant for music; it was, in fact, what we should call an opera libretto. But while the text has been reprinted countless times, the music has been lost. The name of the protagonist (Baccio Ugolino) is recorded, but not that of the composer. The nature of the lost music can be guessed at; it was composed in a simple kind of polyphonic style that ruled out the effect of declamation. The less lyrical parts of Poliziano's text were probably spoken. The choral pieces consisted of the part-songs *(frottole)* then in vogue, which were a simple, harmonic kind of madrigal. The solo music even was polyphonic, the voice part being one strand in a texture of songlike parts woven by the lute and other instruments.

This fifteenth-century *Orfeo* has sometimes been described as the foundation of modern opera. So much cannot be allowed because no development of musical drama ensued, and indeed for a century the trend of music led away from the vividness and directness of effective dramatic utterance. The glory of Italian music in the sixteenth century was the elaborate polyphonic style which had been taken over from the Flemings and refined and embellished to the last degree. This style of involved part-writing, purely vocal in inspiration, and impersonal and ideally beautiful in effect, was and remains the most admirable for liturgical service. It also gave rise to a secondary but exquisite secular form, the madrigal. But in the polyphonic Mass, motet and madrigal the individual was sunk. The new Florentines — the circle *(camerata)* of artists and wits who gathered round Giovanni Bardi and Jacopo Corsi* — were dramatists. For their purposes a style was necessary that would

---

* G. Bardi dei Conti Vernio (1534—1612), mathematician and musician, was from 1592 chamberlain (maestro di camera) to the Pope. G. B. Doni indicates that he was the leading spirit in the movement. Corsi was a wealthy Florentine who became the centre of the group after Bardi had gone to Rome. He tried his hand at setting parts of Rinuccini's *Dafne*.

enhance the individual. The words must stand out, the characters must stand out, at all costs.

The librettist of the first Florentine operas was Ottavio Rinuccini. His subjects, Daphne, Eurydice, Ariadne, were those of the court pastorals that had been in vogue for more than a hundred years. Wherein lay the peculiarity of the new operatic form? It lay in the style of the music — the *stile rappresentativo*. The poets of the time, notably Tasso, resented the loss of their words in the polyphonic maze. As W. S. Gilbert later on put it —

> "No single word is ever heard
> When singers sing in chorus."

The new movement arose not among celebrated musicians but among poets and dilettanti who inspired minor composers to put their theories into practice. No doubt there are in the previous music of the century hints to be found of the new recitative; and in all the centuries there must have been solo singing which allowed of the expression of the singer's personality. But others had been of lyrical character. The Florentine recitative was, so to say, a musical prose, and it arose from a new idea, that of forming music on the basis of the inflexions of dramatic speech.

The first composers in this style were Emilio Cavalieri (1550-1602), Vincenzo Galilei (1533-1591), Peri, and Giulio Caccini (1550-1618). Cavalieri wrote recitatives "after the antique manner"* in a pastoral and an oratorio, but he composed no opera. Galilei, a fanatical enemy of the polyphonic school, declaimed extracts from Dante and Jeremiah to his own music, accompanying himself on the viol. Peri and Caccini were both professional singers. Peri's *Dafne* has been lost, but we have his *Euridice,* at the first production of which in 1600 the composer sang as Orpheus — with overwhelming effect. Caccini also composed an *Euridice.*** Their works have not lived; but the recitative of their invention (which in the first place depended largely on the art of an exceptional singer with the actor's gift) was taken up by greater musicians, was enriched melodically, was reinforced by accompaniments according to the harmonic and orchestral resources of different generations, and became a form in which music could unite with dramatic action and yet preserve its rights. For purposes of comic dialogue

* Quoted by Rolland (Lavignac's Encyclopédie).
** Edited by R. Eitner, Berlin, 1881. Eitner's collection includes Gagliano's *Dafne,* and works by Cavalli, Cesti and others to be mentioned.

recitative (stripped, for rapidity's sake, of accompaniment, and indeed of all but a modicum of music)* was employed in Italy, while in other lands its place was taken by spoken words. For emotional and tragic uses recitative was almost immediately enriched by the first great musician of the theatre, Claudio Monteverdi (b. Cremona 1567, d. Venice 1643), who also imported into opera lyric song, dance and pageantry.

But first, in parenthesis, a word is due to Orazio Vecchi (1551-1605), whose *Amfiparnasso* (Modena, 1594) has often been called an opera with polyphonic music. It is hardly that; but the fourteen madrigals are consecutive, illustrating a farcical story typical of the *commedia dell' arte* or harlequinade, and the work has been effectively produced in London (1946) as a marionette opera, with the madrigals sung behind the stage. An early composer of true opera was Marco da Gagliano (1575-1642), a Florentine, who set Rinuccini's *Dafne* according to the new theories, but with a certain leaning towards lyricism.

Monteverdi's surviving operas are *Orfeo*

---

* *Recitativo secco* was first employed in Marazzoli's *Chi soffre speri* (Rome, 1639). See H. Goldschmidt: Ital. Oper im 17 Jahrh., 1904.

(1607), *Ulisse* (1641), and *L'Incoronazione di Poppea* (1642). All three have been performed in England in recent years.* The lost operas included an *Arianna* (1608), of which a noble fragment survives. There exists also a dramatic cantata, *Il Combattimento di Tancredi e di Clorinda,* which has lately been performed. This piece is famous for the use of the instrumental tremolo, one of Monteverdi's inventions. It is typical of the period that this novel effect resulted from the composer's attempt to reproduce in music the pyrrhic foot of Greek verse. Monteverdi was a man of lively genius, curious, open-minded, impressionable; a master of traditional technics, yet ready for any experiment. He opened his art to many new elements. After 300 years we still feel vitality in his music. In ingenuous grace and freshness of poetic fancy it is the equivalent of fourteenth-century Florentine painting. *Orfeo* is in the main an essay in the new Florentine *stile rappresentativo,* which we see at its finest in such pages as the messenger's tale of Eurydice's death. Tragic recitative was to know great heights in the next centuries; but in Monteverdi — thanks to the waywardness of the tonal sequences (the new

* The first and third at Oxford in 1925 and 1927; the second by the B.B.C. in 1928.

system of tonality being not yet set hard and
fast) — it has a peculiar delicacy and surprise.
Orfeo is not all recitative. Monteverdi was no
rigid theorist. He relieved the severity of the
declamation with ballet, madrigal and song.
Act I. is indeed masque rather than drama. In
Orpheus's song of triumph is the germ of operatic aria. Monteverdi did not command the
sustained grandeur or power of climax which
came naturally to a later generation and which
easily turned to pompousness. But his *Orfeo*
charms us with a primitive delicacy and truth
of accent. *Ulisse,* with its greater variety of
characterization, stands between *Orfeo* and the
astonishing *Poppea,* which must have engrossed
the Venetian public if only by the lively interest
of the plot and the personages. *Poppea* represents a true reconciliation between music and
drama. The action is rapid, the characters
numerous and clear-cut. There is the sensuous
Nero, the jealous and tragic Octavia, the noble
Seneca; and then in the margin, so to say, of the
action such witty trifles as the love-making between the page and the maid of honour. The
scene is crowded, half a dozen passionate characters are in conflict, and the music defines all.
The score is full of songs, but they are terse, are
still ditties rather than arias (though the coming

of the aria is clearly pointed), and do not exert
the weighty pressure that was later to produce
the "grand manner". It is clear how the composer (who was seventy-five) delighted in the
promptings of his vivid libretto; and Oxford
audiences know how interesting is the result.
But there is no need to exaggerate and, with
Henry Prunières,* to drag in Shakespeare and
Titian for comparisons.

In the meantime the new dramatic music had
made its influence felt on the composition of
sacred music; if polyphonic church music was
still written, the style was felt to be archaic and
assumed. The cantata was a seventeenth-century
derivation from opera. It was at first an operatic
scena, detachable and suitable for performance
without stage action, like the Lament from
Monteverdi's *Arianna,* which had an immense
vogue in the music-loving homes of Italy. Such
scenes were then particularly composed first for
domestic performance and then for the church.
The cantata in its turn, by the end of the seventeenth century, came to influence the opera, in-
ducing in Scarlatti and Handel that stately
movement and deliberation which cause the
operas of those composers to strike the modern
spectator as concerts in costume.

* Prunières's Monteverdi. London, 1926.

Rome, Venice and, later, Naples saw the most
brilliant developments of the first century of
opera. Under the patronage of the Barberini the
Roman school was very active between 1623-
1644. The leading musicians were Mazzocchi,
Landi, Marazzoli, Rossi. The Barberini theatre
accommodated 3,500. The principal librettist
was Cardinal Rospigliosi (later Pope Clement
IX). The Roman operas developed comic relief
and also the use of elaborate machinery for
spectacular effects. This brilliant period was
brief, thanks to the more austere policy of a new
Pope.

At Venice, meanwhile, the first public opera-
house was opened (1637). Later the city could
boast seventeen opera-houses. There flourished
a succession of remarkable composers. Cavalli,
Cesti, Legrenzi, Stradella, Caldara, Lotti were
all more or less connected with Venice.

Francesco Cavalli (1599-1676) learnt from
Monteverdi and probably influenced his master's
Poppea. He composed thirty-nine operas. He
possessed a strong melodic vein. His vocal line
indicates the developing technics of Italian singers, technics which were, before the end of the
century, to become an end in themselves and a
danger to the dramatic interest. Cavalli's *Giasone*
(1649) contains, alongside a striking Incanta-

tion for Medea, comic scenes for an old maid in quest of a husband and also for an absurd stammerer. Opera, with Cavalli, has still a primitive charm. Cesti (1620-1669), a Franciscan monk, won fame in Austria. His *Pomo d'Oro,* in sixty-seven scenes, cost a king's ransom to produce at Vienna in 1666. The interest lay in the spectacle and in charming songs. Stradella (1645-1682), a wayward genius, influenced Handel and Scarlatti. Himself a singing teacher, he flattered the virtuosity of singers. He died young, assassinated by the Venetian Contarini, following his elopement with a lady connected with that family.

We come to a great musician: Alessandro Scarlatti (1659-1725), who composed about one hundred and twenty-five operas, some for Rome, some for Florence and Venice, and many for Naples. Opera had reached Naples from Venice in the 1650's. Provenzale (1610-1704) was the first Neapolitan opera composer. Scarlatti was at Naples from 1684-1702, 1708-1718 and 1722-1725. With Scarlatti we reach the period of classical music; but his operas must be called archaic, since not one has held the stage. Librettos seem to have been mechanically written for him and he accepted them as mechanically. From an unfailing source of melody he would distribute between the puppets of each piece some fifty arias. The shape of the aria was now tending to become invariable — the aria *da capo,* the repeat being the singer's opportunity for improvised ornamentations. There was hardly any choral or concerted writing; the orchestra rarely had an independent interest.

Opera, now conventionalized, was as far removed from the "primitives" as were Pope's couplets from Elizabethan exuberance. The audience of the day expected to be pleased in an expected way. The forms of opera and of its component parts, overture, recitative, aria, were regularly classified. The noble characters, whatever their vicissitudes, kept to a rigid school of manners. The comic characters who mocked them in the *intermezzi* had more latitude. They were descendants of the comedy of masks. In Neapolitan opera they came to have more importance than at Venice, and early in the eighteenth century they branched off into independent comic opera *(opera buffa),* leaving *opera seria* in undisturbed majesty. Scarlatti wrote one comic opera, *Il Trionfo dell' Onore,* which should be revived. His grand operas are appreciated to-day, and deserve to be more appreciated, as repositories of admirable songs, conventional in form, but charmingly melodious and adorned

with a wealth of fancy — the musical equivalent, as Dent says, of baroque architecture.
"Consciously or unconsciously, Scarlatti did as
much as any composer to bring about the de-
gradation of the musical drama that preceded
the reforms of Gluck; but . . . his sins with regard
to musical drama were far outweighed by his
priceless contribution of the development of
pure music" (Dent: Alessandro Scarlatti, London, 1905).

The ballet was an established French Court
entertainment on which Italian Opera made its
influence felt quite early in the seventeenth
century. Then Mazarin in the 1640's brought
Italian composers to Paris, where Luigi Rossi's
Orfeo, a fine example of early opera, was
produced in 1647. French hostility to the Italians
on political grounds hindered development; but
the first French opera, Cambert's Pomone, was
produced in 1671. This led the way for Lully
(b. Florence 1632, d. Paris 1687) the first great
name in French opera: a foreigner, like several
musicians who have greatly contributed to
French opera (thus Gluck, Cherubini, Rossini,
Meyerbeer), but in style a thorough Frenchman.
For fifteen years Lully wrote ballets, and in the
last fifteen years of his life operas, notably Cad-
mus (1673), Alceste (1674), Thésée (1675),

Armide (1686). The Lullian opera was an elaborate entertainment, solidly based on Quinault's excellent librettos: its backbone a solemn and emphatic recitative, closely related to the contemporary declamation of tragedy, and musically rather dry; its adornments numerous, including buffo scenes, dances, processions. Lully lacked melodious charm; his harmony was plain and unadventurous. His operas are the musical expression of the pomp of Louis XIV's court. They made no headway abroad, but they were played in France for a century. And nearly half a century after Lully's death Rameau's first opera *Hippolyte* (1733) was censured for its departure from his style.

Rameau (1683-1764) wrote operas only in the latter part of his life. *Castor et Pollux* (1737), his masterpiece, has been revived in our times. He was a distinguished musician, his harmony richer than Lully's, his orchestral writing more developed. His operas contain choruses and ballets, as those of his Italian contemporaries did not. While nothing like the magnificence of Handel's genius must be looked for in Rameau his music is finely rococo in the best sense, inventive and aristocratic.

The masque was an Italian entertainment that took root in England under Henry VIII.

and flourished especially under the first Stuart kings. The splendour of the poetry of Elizabethan drama, far surpassing the Continental theatre, perhaps militated against English opera. Music on the English stage was used incidentally. The first English opera,* *The Siege of Rhodes* (1656), was the outcome of the Puritans' proscription of the spoken drama. Its text was by Davenant; the music was principally by Lawes, Cooke and Locke, and is now wholly lost. But works by those composers survive, notably an opera-like masque, *Cupid and Death*, of 1659 (text by Shirley, music by Locke and Christopher Gibbons), whose recitative points to Purcell. Locke's *Psyche* (1673) was an imitation of a work of Lully's. He was no great musician; but another work of the period, Blow's *Venus and Adonis*, which shows the masque developing into opera, is attractive while naive, and has been revived in our times.

Henry Purcell (1658-1695) was a pupil of Blow's. He was the bright genius of the age, and his early death was a loss comparable with that of Mozart or Schubert. Purcell wrote two operas:

---

*E. J. Dent's Foundations of English Opera (1928) is the standard work on the period.

Dido and Aeneas (1689) and *King Arthur** (1691); and in the incidental music and masques he provided for contemporary plays and adaptations of Shakespeare there are stretches of true operatic composition, notably in *The Fairy Queen, Bonduca, The Tempest* and *The Indian Queen. Dido* was written for a girls' school at Chelsea. It is a little work, but its short span is vivid with musical response and invention, all astonishingly varied, original and moving. Out of Italian recitative Purcell made an admirable means of English expression, extremely musical and no less faithful to our language. Dido's Lament is immortal music. The brilliant dawn was, however, illusory. The day of English opera was to be of an almost gleamless grey.

The first German opera is considered to have been Heinrich Schütz's *Dafne* (1627). But the influx of Italian opera, which was the delight of the principal German Courts during the seventeenth and eighteenth centuries, left little room for native art. Only in republican Hamburg there arose towards the end of the seventeenth century (1678) a noteworthy school, illustrated by the names of Kusser (Cousser), Keiser, Han-

* Text by Dryden, who had also written an opera text, *Albion and Albanius*, for the French Master of the King's Music, Louis Grabu, an inferior composer.

del, Mattheson, Telemann. Reinhard Keiser
(1673-1739) composed more than a hundred
operas for Hamburg (eight in one year, 1709). A
strongly Italianate style prevailed. Keiser did not
hesitate to make use of a composite German and
Italian text. *Octavia* (1705) and *Almira* (1706),
written to rival Handel's *Almira* and *Nerone*
(1705), are considered his masterpieces. German
opera at Hamburg succumbed to the Italians in
1740. Hamburg had the musical talent but
not the literary and theatrical culture (German
literature being then almost at its nadir) to rise
to the opportunity and create a national opera.
Keiser's work is forgotten, save for the influence
it had on Bach and Handel.

George Frederic Handel (1685-1759) went
to Hamburg when he was eighteen and composed for that stage three operas, one of which,
Almira, written on a mixed German and Italian
text, survives. In 1707 he went to Italy, and
composed *Rodrigo* for Florence and *Agrippina*
for Venice; and in 1710 he reached England.
Rinaldo (1711) was the first of his long series
of London operas. These number about thirty-
eight, all written to Italian texts. A smaller
number of works composed to English texts,
such as *Esther, Acis* and *Galatea* and *Semele,*
are operas in all but name; they form a link

between the operas proper and the English oratorios, which occupied Handel in his latter years. The last of the Italian operas was *Deidamia* (1740).

A prodigious genius poured itself into these numerous and lengthy works, which were sometimes produced three in a year. The musical style of Handel's operas is radically an Italian style: blunted by the composer's lack of intimacy with the language he was setting, and stiffened and enriched by his sturdy and exuberant character. Handel was at once composer and impresario; in the latter capacity he suffered the ups and downs inseparable from the promotion of an expensive entertainment in a foreign language. A sentimental view has too often been taken of Handel's reverses. A German writing Italian operas for a London audience was an anomaly; but the English Handel of the oratorios stood on solid earth. The operas fell almost at once into desuetude. For generations they were remembered only by isolated arias. Of late the historical imagination has attempted to come to the rescue, but it is a hopeless cause. The formality of the action in these operas and the superhuman nobility of the characters represent too faithfully the ideal of an extinct society. Handel's heroes, and Rameau's, are rather semi-divinities than men in the invariable stateliness of their utterance, as in their sumptuous bewiggedness that submerges the individual in a type. They are the ideal of an aristocratic age; they represent the prince, the nobleman, superb to a degree at which their humanity is barely discernible.

Handel dwarfs Rameau; yet in an age like ours, when the art of the dance is more attached to tradition than is that of song, Rameau's ballet music enjoys a better chance of justice than Handel's opera arias. The original effect of these is irretrievable through the disappearance of the Italian eunuchs whose prodigious voices (combining the ranges of tenor and soprano) were throughout the early classical period the craze of all Europe. No aria was too long, no repetitions redundant when a leading castrato occupied the stage. That type of voice — round and sweet and at the same time wonderfully sonorous — was an almost unimaginable factor in the dramatic music of the age.

III

THE CLASSICAL PERIOD

ITALY remained during the eighteenth century the true home of opera. There it was the national entertainment, it may be said to have been a staple industry; and the school of Italian singing was unrivalled in Europe. But enormous though the production of operatic music was in Italy, and delightful the talents of a long succession of composers, the most striking geniuses did not belong there (though schooled in Italian art) but to lands where opera presented problems of acclimatization, where the material (language, dramatic substance) was, so to say, still raw, thus offering a challenge to the musician's invention and organizing power.

Italian composers overran Europe. Buononcini (1675-1726) flourished in London, Porpora (1686-1767) in London, Dresden and Vienna, Jommelli (1714-1774) in Vienna and Stuttgart, Piccini (1728-1800) in Paris, Paisiello (1714-1816) in Paris and St. Petersburg, Cimarosa (1749-1801) in St. Petersburg and Vienna. Salieri (1750-1825) spent half a century at

Vienna. Cherubini (1760-1842) settled in Paris.
But Cherubini belongs to a different period; and
a condition of his choice was then (as it would
not have been a generation before) that he became virtually French. The typical peregrinating
Italian opera-composer of the eighteenth century
carried to the ends of Europe his fashionable,
decorative art like a little piece of Italy. Very
few are the works that survive (like the inter-
mezzo *La Serva Padrona* of Pergolesi, 1710-
1736, and Cimarosa's sparkling *Matrimonio
Segreto* of 1792) of that vast quantity of music.
The composers seem to have aimed at nothing
but the ephemeral. Where Italian comic opera
(opera buffa) of the 18th century survives im-
mortally is in the work of a non-Italian. As for
formal heroic opera *(opera seria)*, it maintained
existence almost until the end of the century as
an embellishment of court life, but had long before this been in fact superseded by a more
vigorous heir.

The Italian influence subdued and absorbed
some foreign musicians, such as Hasse (1699-
1783) who, though a Hamburger by birth and
principally a Dresdener by domicile, must be
counted not a German but an Italian composer.
He enjoyed a great reputation from London to
Naples. His music (a vast mass) is, however,

forgotten. His fame was soon eclipsed by that of a contemporary who, while far from being the most refined of musicians, had the originality of character (let us call it genius) to explore a new way, and a fruitful one; to add a new province to his art; to stimulate music by a fresh contact with life.

The course of an art is not properly regarded as an evolutionary progress, nor one achievement as a stage towards another more complete. Yet progress is not to be at all times denied. Life changes; all things are in flux. The conventions that are wings for one generation of artists may become a cage for the next. Gluck is not necessarily to be called a finer musician than Scarlatti or Rameau, but for his generation he was the man who broke down conventional barriers and showed the view beyond, he was the progressive genius and as such the admiration of his age. His operas are the earliest that remain current in the repertory.

Christolph Willibald Gluck (1714-1787) spent his life writing Italian and, towards the end, French operas; but he remained German at least to this degree — that although he did not write professedly or characteristically German music he saw the established Italian operatic conventions at a certain distance, saw their proportions to other things, and saw them not as an irrefragable dogma and not all-applicable. Gluck wrote some fifty operatic works. His fame is based on the five French operas of his latest period. They were: *Iphigénie en Aulide* (Paris, 1774), *Orphée* (1774), *Alceste* (1776), *Armide* (1777), *Iphigénie en Tauride* (1779). These works all incorporated many pages from Gluck's Italian operas; and two, *Orphée* and *Alceste*, were indeed revisions of his *Orfeo ed Euridice* (Vienna, 1762) and *Alceste* (Vienna, 1767). *Orfeo* marked the turning point, and the published score of the Italian *Alceste* contained the historical dedicatory epistle in which Gluck laid down the principles of his reformation of the opera. Herein he declared it his object to strip dramatic music of the "abuses introduced by the perverse vanity of singers"; to restore music "to its true function of seconding the effect of the poetry and plot, without interrupting the action or overlaying it with superfluous ornament". The whole letter is a classic. We may well wonder how it came that the sturdy, rather simple and extremely successful Gluck should, when he was nearing fifty, have adopted this revolutionary aesthetic, for revolutionary it was and no less. There was no one cause but a complex of causes. Ernest Newman says:

"From all we know of him — his birth, his ancestry, the early conditions of his life, his later relations with men — it is clear that much of his forthright spirit of innovation was simply the intellectual expression of a healthy, vigorous, independent, unsophisticated nature, forcing itself, in spite of all opposition and of every seduction, into the way that was most natural to it."*

There is also the fact that many of these ideas were in the air — had indeed long been in the air. At the beginning of the century Keiser had expressed something of Gluck's aesthetic in declaring his purpose to be "the depiction of the passions in their natural nakedness" and also in proclaiming the importance of the orchestral instruments as a means of expression. In the crystallizing of his ideas Gluck owed not a little to the librettist of *Orfeo,* the Italian poet Calzabigi, whose text, differing much from the conventional texts of the day, set the musician a new problem, and who, moreover, had strong views of his own on the proprieties of musical

* E. Newman: Gluck and the Opera, 1895.
Consult also Alfred Einstein's *Gluck* (London, 1936), where a share in the credit for Gluck's reforms is allowed to Count Durazzo, intendant of the Viennese theatres in 1754—64.

treatment. Years later Calzabigi made extravagant claims for himself; nonetheless, it is certain that the literature and the philosophy of the day ("the return to nature"), reaching the musician through the suggestions of this or that man of letters, were agents in the new development of music. The art was enclosed; it was languishing. Gluck's labours in those years 1762-1779 left it invigorated, and generations later the influence of those labours was still not exhausted. Berlioz sat at his feet and worked out the implications of his art of scoring as Wagner worked out his dramatic theories.

Gluck (who sought, so he said, "to be a painter or poet rather than music-maker") aimed at a new truth of dramatic expression in opera. This meant first a wider variety of invention on the musician's part. It meant the break-up of the *da capo* air. It meant the enrichment of the recitative, the abolition of the old harpsichord-accompanied recitative, and an interest in all the declamation equal to that of the purely lyrical movements. In practice Gluck was unable to carry out all his principles. But what we notice first in the five masterpieces is the individuality of each (excepting, perhaps, the first *Iphigenia,* which, for all its magnificent contents, has not too clear a general character).

Orphée is a pathetic mythological idyll, delicate and remote; the long-drawn pathos of *Alceste* is quite different, direct and human. *Armide* abounds in variety, suited to the meandering romance of the story. The second *Iphigénie* is very noble, severe, homogeneous, and perhaps the finest work of the series. In the revision of *Orfeo* the hero's part, at first written for male alto (eunuch), was arranged for tenor. Modern producers restore the alto part, allotting it, however, to a woman. *Alceste,* in the French revision, was brought nearer to Euripides by the introduction of Herakles. The merry-making at the close of both operas, as likewise in the first *Iphigénie,* is a flaw. Gluck was a strong man, but was not strong enough to rise to all his ideals. The happy ending was a convention he could not break down, nor could he withstand the Parisians' demand for immoderate shows of dancing (a ballet in each act). At the same time, something must be said for the contributions made by French tradition to these masterpieces. The text of the first *Iphigénie* was adapted from Racine; that of *Armide* was Quinault's, which Lully had set. Minor setbacks and polemics apart, Gluck's career in Paris was triumphant. He was recognized as the successor of Lully and Rameau. He glorified French opera, which from the musical point of view had been rather dry. But French opera had a superior literary tradition, and this helped to incite Gluck to his characteristic vividness and nobility.

What of Gluck's operas to-day? The innovations have long ago ceased to be recognizable except by the student. His art lives by force of the classic grandeur of his subjects, by the sincerity of his melody, by the effect of his simple but inspired orchestral strokes. Inequality is felt, and some dulness — for, dramatist that he was, invention would suddenly fail when the text ceased to enthrall him. Gluck remains one of the giants of music; and the five masterpieces are pillars of those houses of opera where the art is most seriously esteemed and cultivated.

A curious minor activity of Gluck's Viennese period was the composition of French comic operas. The *opéra comique* became in the second half of the eighteenth century the most characteristic form of French musical composition. It was more or less the equivalent of the Italian *opera buffa*, the German *Singspiel*, the English ballad opera. But nowhere was the colloquial recitative (*secco* or "plain") of the Italians acclimatized. The various forms of comic opera fell back on spoken dialogue, or else were simply comedies interspersed with songs. The convention was precarious, but French liveliness and taste maintained it very prettily for some generations. The little masters of the eighteenth century included Philidor (1726-1795), Monsigny (1729-1817), and Grétry (1741-1813). But the mixture of speech and song can with certainty be used only for modest effect, without the pretension of capturing the spectator's whole imagination, or for out-and-out frivolity. The moment the musician sets out to impose himself seriously the use of speech is a derogation. The spoken dialogue in the operas of Beethoven and Weber is atoned for by the grandeur of the music of those masters; but in itself it is (like the weaknesses of the librettos they adopted) but an indication that German opera was at its beginnings, and that the greatest of musical geniuses could not at a stroke solve the whole of the aesthetic problem. Music did not go on tolerating the infringement of its rights. In the course of the nineteenth century speech became swallowed up in music in operas of genuine pretensions, even in France, where a State institution sheltered the traditions. At the Opéra Comique in Paris no opéra comique would today be accepted.

* * * *

After Gluck came Mozart (1756-1791).*
Again an Austrian subject, Italian-trained.
Human history is not like a comet's predictable
course. Impredictable genius brings about all
kinds of diversions. Were the old forms of Italian opera effete? Mozart arrived to shed a new
radiance on its conventional patterns. So far
from pressing along Gluck's path, away from
the Italian style, he set his genius to serve traditional *opera seria* and *opera buffa*, aiming at no
unprecedented novelty, but simply giving a final
and matchless expression to the spirit of his century. Apart from juvenile and unfinished works,
and the one-act operetta, *Der Schauspieldirektor*,
Mozart's operas are the following:

Idomeneo (Munich, 1781), *Die Entführung
aus dem Serail* (Vienna, 1782), *Le Nozze di
Figaro* (Vienna, 1786), *Don Giovanni* (Prague,
1787), *Così fan tutte* (Vienna, 1790), *Die Zauberflöte* (Vienna, 1791), *La Clemenza di Tito*
(Prague, 1791). The first and last of these are
Italian serious operas, the third, fourth and fifth
are Italian comic operas, the second and sixth
German ballad operas. But this classifying does
not carry us far. *La Clemenza di Tito,* hastily
written (in eighteen days) to a libretto by Meta-

* Consult E. J. Dent's Mozart's Operas, London,
1913.

stasio, at a moment when Mozart would more willingly have given all his thoughts to the *Requiem* and to *Die Zauberflöte,* retains less interest for us than the others; but every one of those others is in its way unique, every one immortal. To vivify the frigid libretto of *Idomeneo* (which is about a warrior-king of Crete, who on his return from the Trojan wars unwittingly promises his son as a sacrifice to the gods), Mozart brought a passionate sympathy with human feelings and vicissitudes together with a musical style of the purest Italian elegance, strengthened by an assiduous practice of instrumental composition. *Die Entführung* dates from a period when the Viennese Court was inclined to encourage German opera at the expense of the Italian supremacy. It was a brilliant and charming piece of work, which at one stroke bridged the space between obscure and humdrum German comic opera and the dazzling Italian style. Music, was, however, Mozart's preoccupation — not movements. His next three operas were Italian. Here he enjoyed the collaboration of a capital librettist, Lorenzo da Ponte.

It is good that Cimarosa's *Matrimonio Segreto* should have survived, not only for the sake of its own gaiety, but also because we can measure

by it the departures made by Mozart in *Figaro*
and *Don Giovanni* from normal contemporary
work. No aesthetic theory, but the composer's
acute sensibility worked against the traditions,
with the result that neither *Figaro* nor *Don
Giovanni* makes simply the bright and bustling
effect that an audience of that day expected.
Figaro became softer, more sweet and sunny,
than the plot (which indeed a turn or two of the
screw might have made tragic) had indicated;
and *Don Giovanni,* which might have been
reckless farce, took on dark hues and sinister
shadows. In the one opera the faithful loves of
Figaro and Susanna (both so gay, yet so honest)
and the Countess's tender heart have half eclipsed for Mozart the cruelty which is the spring of
the action. In *Don Giovanni* it is just the other
way: the gaiety is only a sardonic gleam seen on
the suffering which Don Juan's fascination
spreads like the spell of an evil eye. *Figaro,* so
radiant for all the peril of tears, is the more
perfect: "the most perfect opera in all classical
music" (D. F. Tovey). Song after song is a direct
apparition of music's self — which astonishingly
takes on all kinds of human characteristics, yet
remains divine. The ensemble pieces and finales,
in which Viennese symphonic art is wedded to
Italian stagecraft, seem to spring into being at

the wave of a wand. Yet of the two operas
Don Giovanni may be considered the more won-
derful. Take the opera page by page, and there
is nowhere an eccentricity or a striving after
romantic mystery. Yet an effect of singularity
remains, surviving many of the poetical fantasies
that were about to crop up everywhere in
Europe. It is as though Mozart was almost in-
nocent of the result. The cruelty of the Italian
comedy was conventional; the despairing passion was not unconventional. The composer
treated both these elements exquisitely but, as
it were, separately; and a contemporary critic
might have said that the treatment of the latter
was unduly serious in the circumstances. That
very difference is what gives *Don Giovanni* its
peculiarity and subtlety — reached, as it seems,
by accident, but a divine accident. Imperfections
in the construction of the opera are visible
enough; and yet the indifferent characterization
of Don Ottavio and a certain perfunctoriness in
the treatment of Don Giovanni himself, which
have sometimes been made much of, turn out
not to be faults at all. They are simply Ottavio
and Giovanni as Leporello saw or remembered
them. Leporello is the most vivid person of the
piece, the most fully realized and solidly established. All the rest are more or less dreamlike,

and the action is dreamlike. The difficulty of those who, while admiring the opera to the last iota, are troubled by its loose ends and shaky structure, disappears if *Don Giovanni* is recognized as Leporello's dream. The 19th century could not relish the sardonic effect of the cheerful finale to the second act, and brought the opera to an end with the catastrophe. But it is a mistake to lose any element of this dream-fantasy. The fineness of Mozart's style demands that men shall keep on calling his art divine, but of course that is only an expression; the style drew from thoroughly human sources and in the operas very frequently from visible things — as in "Madamina", where, between Leporello's phrases, the orchestra plainly imitates the knave's flick in unrolling the infamous scroll.

If *Così fan tutte* (called in English after its alternative Italian title "The School for Lovers") is another dream, as we have sometimes seen it presented, it is a strictly logical one. The subject is slight; the opera is long. But Mozart's art was the most subtle means there has ever been for the expression of the sentimental affections, and *Così fan tutte* is not too long for his range and fineness. Two young lovers, egged on by an elderly cynic, resolve to test the constancy of their mistresses. They pretend to depart for the wars, then turn up to woo the ladies in the disguise of Oriental potentates. The cynic wins his bet; but it is a comedy and all ends well. We know not whether to admire more the range — from superb parody of the heroic manner (in "Come scoglio"), gaiety more or less heartless, tenderness more or less unaffected, to the bliss of "E nel tuo, nel mio bicchiero'" — or the infallible tact with which the whole is kept within the frame of a high elegance. Though farce is only just round the corner this supremely well-bred fineness makes for an effect almost of seriousness. The 18th century bequeathed nothing more exquisite.

Mozart shines in another aspect in his last opera, *The Magic Flute*. The source was not aristocratic but popular — a fairytale with monsters, transformation scenes and comic relief. Considered as literature, the libretto (believed to have been written in the main by C. W. Gieseke) is, on the face of it, irresponsible enough, yet it served Mozart as the scaffolding for a temple of music. We look into the clear deep pools of *The Magic Flute* and literary prejudices disappear in wonder.*

* Busoni once wrote to a critic: "You should have adduced the example, if there is one, of a better libretto than that of the *Zauberflöte*".

Mozart was the born opera composer ready with the best possible music for anything. But there was more to it than that. *The Magic Flute* libretto had the merit of interesting the composer deeply, concealing as it did an allegory touching a conflict of old and new beliefs in which he felt a lively concern. The Queen of Night, jealous and intolerant, stands for old and dark ways of thought, Sarastro for a new enlightenment. Mozart was an ardent freemason in his later years. There can be no doubt that the glow of his conviction helped to idealize for him Tamino's adventures and ordeal. The plot, on the face of it so dull, took on a wealth of spiritual beauty and suggestion. In composing the *Zauberflöte* Mozart made himself humble. To approach Sarastro he divested himself of his learning and his wit. The new-found peace of mind of the convert is felt in the music — the simplest and most serene of all great music — associated with the high priest and the mysteries. Mozart is like a child again in this truly religious composition of *Die Zauberflöte*. It is all matchlessly beautiful. Tenderness and charity so abound as to embrace the comic relief, till before the end we are not sure whether there is not something angelic about the feathered Papageno, the preposterous bird-catcher. Only the shrill songs of the Queen recall the past and the world of false illusion.

Mozart's death at thirty-five was the worst disaster music has ever suffered. The new age needed him. Great men, indeed, but relatively clumsy ones, were to forge the operas of the coming century. No one else possessed quite such a quickness of life, such a sensibility; never was there another such instrument of music as Mozart's mind.

*   *   *   *

Beethoven (1770-1827) in his youth played the violin in the opera orchestra at Bonn, his native town, where the repertory embraced a great variety of Italian, French and German works, including Mozart's *Entführung*, *Figaro* and *Don Giovanni*. He composed a ballet for Bonn, and a second ballet, *Prometheus*, for Vienna (1801). Projects for operatic composition haunted Beethoven all his life. Schikaneder, the impresario of *Die Zauberflöte*, took steps to obtain an opera from him. At different times in his life he thought over operas on the subjects of Macbeth, Lear, Romeo and Juliet, Alfred the Great, Bacchus, Romulus and Remus, and many more. In 1806, after the production of *Fidelio*,

he proposed to the managers of the Vienna
Court Opera an arrangement by which he would
compose a grand opera for them every year.
Quite late in his career he contemplated long
and seriously a·*Melusine* by Grillparzer, the best
dramatic poet of Vienna. Yet *Fidelio* remained
the only opera Beethoven was to leave us. The
difficulty, the impossibility, experienced by
Beethoven in suiting himself with a libretto was
due in part to the poverty of the Germans in
literary talent and craftsmanship. German literature was a new growth. It could boast already
a man of first-rate genius, but in general culture there was no comparison between German
letters and music. Vienna in particular, where
the musical life was intense, possessed in Beethoven's young days no literary traditions or
talent. Then Beethoven himself was difficult.
He was capable of rejecting, even if they had
come his way, any number of useful librettos on
the ground of personal indifference or antipathy.
This was a new phenomenon in music; it was
the new individualism which proclaimed the
modern age. Before, music had in all its different degrees been a matter of craftsmanship.
Now it was to be the expression of the artist's
self. Towards the end of his life Beethoven said
to a would-be librettist:

"You'll have trouble with me! I care little what category the works belong to, so the material be attractive to me. But it must be something I can take up with sincerity and love. I could not compose works like *Don Giovanni* and *Figaro*. They are repugnant to me. I could not have chosen such subjects; they are too frivolous for me!" (Thayer, iii 201.)

Beethoven once declared that the two best opera texts ever written were those of Cherubini's *Deux Journées* (1800) and Spontini's *Vestale* (1807). *Fidelio* was adapted by Sonnleithner, secretary of the Vienna Court Theatre, from the *Léonore* of the author of *Les Deux Journées*, Bouilly. Cherubini's *Lodoïska* (1791) reached Vienna in 1802 and had much success. Beethoven always expressed high regard for Cherubini's serious and substantial art; at the same time he was convinced of his own surpassing ability. *Fidelio* was composed in 1805 and performed on November 20. This was a week after the occupation of Vienna by the French. The Court and the aristocracy had fled. French soldiery filled the theatre. The opera was a failure. With certain changes (the three acts reduced to two) it was revived in the next year. A quarrel between the composer and the director of the theatre stopped its career. Then in

1814 there was again a revision and a new production.

Beethoven had not the luck to find the librettist he needed nor the aptitude to think out a dramatic plan for himself. *Fidelio* strikes one in the eye with its imperfections. There is no drama but only a dramatic situation. The opening scenes are comic opera, agreeable but irrelevant. The motto of dramatic construction, "Prepare!", is ignored. Pizarro is a villain and Florestan a prisoner; from first to last we know nothing more of them. Yet, even so, Beethoven was not to be frustrated. *Fidelio,* after all, contained something for him; and though we think of it as a fragment it is a fragment greater than the whole achievement of contemporaries. Leonora's pure flame of heroism burns in Beethoven's music for ever.

*　　　*　　　*　　　*

The world of the eighteenth century was in dissolution; the period of romanticism succeeded that of reason, and in Germany, peculiarly victimized by the Napoleonic campaigns, a lively sentiment of nationalism was awakened to give a new quality and colour to the age. Romanticism was a movement of idealization of country against town, mountaineer and peasant against effete citizen, superstition against scepticism. The town welcomed it, as a change. The new fashionable feelings — poetic, patriotic, uncouth, absurd, vital and hopeful — were reflected in the works of Carl Maria von Weber (1786-1826), whose principal operas were *Der Freischütz* (Berlin, 1821), *Euryanthe* (Vienna, 1823), and *Oberon* (London, 1826). Weber, the brilliant and charming troubadour, was born to be the subject of a biographical novel. He was one of the great instinctive musicians. His fancy took fire from the subjects — dank forests, ghosts and fairies, huntsmen, blue-eyed village heroines — with which the Germans were busy nourishing their young literature, in opposition to the classical or Frenchified fare of their fathers.

Weber went to Dresden and dethroned Italian opera. *Der Freischütz* was produced at Berlin and Spontini's glory paled. The opera conquered Europe. In London it was produced at three different theatres simultaneously. "The Demon Hunter" is the usual English title; no literal translation is possible, since the conception of a Freischütz* does not exist in England. Magic,

* i.e., a charmed or bewitched bullet.

with us, went out before firearms came in. In Germany the opera is held in pious affection to this day, so strong is the element of national consciousness that mingles there in the cult of music. To fix the attention on the pure poetry of the work is not easy in face of its puerility. The librettist, Kind, was a barnstormer play-wright. Weber was no clown — he was a man of the world, and a brilliant spokesman of the culture of his time and country — and yet he lavished his music over this *Freischütz* and the confused *Euryanthe*. An evening with the earlier opera affords only a few moments of the poetry which Weber's name suggests, but those few are worth a good deal. There is the magical over-ture, and then such lovely songs as "Durch die Wälder" and "Leise, leise." There is the music for the scene in the haunted glen, astonishing when we think how little there had been in music before Weber to show him the way to such a rendering of landscape and atmosphere. It is astonishing even in an absolute sense; and after all those ejaculations of broken themes and so much mysterious agitation he must be a thick-skinned listener who does not shudder at the orchestra's wild burst into C minor after the moulding of the sixth bullet. There is another interesting element, and it was derived from the

Latin lands. We think of Weber as brilliant no less than romantic. There are often in his work a sparkle and a recklessness that rarely appeared in German music as the century went on. That sparkle is Latin by derivation; but by adoption Weberian, in association with the poetic German use of orchestral instruments and a more tender feeling than the South or the West knew for the sights of nature and the songs of country folk.

Euryanthe was derived from the same source of medieval French poetry as Shakespeare's *Cymbeline.* The heroine is simple as Elsa, her jealous rival as villainous as Ortrud. But although *Euryanthe* in many ways foretells *Lohengrin,* Wagner would not have been satisfied with the far-fetched motive of the secret ring and its ghostly owner. Indeed, peering into *Euryanthe* one fails to find an adequate motive anywhere in the complicated action. This lack Weber overlooked in the general charm he felt in contemplating the era of romantic chivalry, and not only felt but also conveyed in the thrilling overture and other beautiful pages. But it was a serious lack; one sensible human motive would have given the music (and not merely the argument) the stiffening needed to tide it over changes of fashion, for which its general charm

has proved not enough.* The composition of
Euryanthe is remarkable for boldly melodious
declamation, foretelling Wagner's style; remarkable, too, for the use of musical mottos or
leitmotive which were to become the very foundation of Wagner's practice.** Wagner's use of
such mottos in *Lohengrin* was no more developed than Weber's in *Euryanthe.* A difference,
however, lay in the significance of the reference.
Ortrud's fanatical passion for her old gods was a
real motive, a thought to haunt all about her,
a recurring danger. No character in Weber was
so defined, no one's behaviour had such significance; and the eloquence of his mottos has cor-
respondingly less force.

Euryanthe was the one wholly musical opera
Weber wrote. *Oberon,* composed to an English
text (by J. R. Planché), returned to the mixing
of speech and song. The libretto is a fantastic
rigmarole, straggling through numberless scenes.
Though the music contains extraordinary beau-

* An interesting revision was made by R. Lauckner
and D. F. Tovey in 1922.
** The sinister Eglantine's motto is used in true
Wagnerian fashion when in the scene in the third
act it insinuates itself into the orchestra as Euryanthe
names Eglantine to the King as the source of her
woes.

ties, *Oberon* has long been absent from the stage for which it was composed.

*   *   *   *

While the Germans were struggling, now gloriously, now unluckily, with the problems of national opera the Italians pursued an easier path; there was no doubt (there has never been serious doubt there) about what opera was and should be; the traditions were an ancestral domain which the heirs in the successive generations exploited according to their talents. Through the centuries, from Monteverdi and Cavalli down to Puccini, there has been no break in the dynasty of Italian operatic composers. Each was linked to a predecessor, and all enjoyed the practical incitement of a public for whom the opera-house was the national theatre. In every period the doors were open to the man of talent. In the early nineteenth century the triumphant talent was that of Gioachino Rossini (1792-1868) — "the Italian sun," as Heine called him. Rossini began his first opera, *Demetrio,* when he was sixteen, a student at Bologna. *La Cambiale di Matrimonio* was produced at Venice when he was eighteen. In the next eighteen years came thirty-seven operas, tragic and comic, mostly written in a fortnight or three weeks. After *Guillaume Tell* (Paris, 1829) Rossini lived for nearly forty years, but the only further Rossinian opera in that period was *Robert Bruce,* a cento compiled by Niedermayer from half-a-dozen of the master's early works.

The two principal Italian composers of the generation immediately before Rossini were Cherubini (1760-1842) and Spontini (1774-1851), both of whom lived abroad, the former principally in Paris, the latter in Berlin. Cherubini became virtually a French composer, among the considerable but more or less forgotten group who occupied the Paris scene after Gluck's departure; urbane and dignified composers like Méhul (1763-1817) whose comedy was decorous and whose tragic expression was never carried to excess. Cherubini became a great pedagogue, and a pupil of his (and also of Méhul's) was the modest but elegant comic-opera composer Boieldieu (1775-1834), author of *La Dame Blanche,* the model of its class. Spontini's *Vestale* (Paris, 1807) marked a stage in the development of French "grand opéra" — a form of opera due almost entirely to non-French composers. Gluck's prestige remained great in Paris; great, too, was the attraction of full-throated and decorative Italian singing.

French grand opera represented in the earlier part of the 19th century the attempt to combine dramatic vividness with splendid vocal displays, not to speak of the ballets and pageants which always had a great part in French opera. The species had a brilliant social career, but it lacked a consistent musical style, and time has dealt hardly even with its most illustrious examples: Spontini's work mentioned, Auber's *Muette de Portici,* Rossini's *Tell,* and the imposing productions of the remarkable Berlin Jew Giacomo Meyerbeer (1791-1864). But by the time of Meyerbeer's heyday Rossini had retired from the scene.

Towards the end of his life, having composed a Petite Messe Solennelle, Rossini jotted down at the end of the score a somewhat impertinent note addressed to the Deity, in which he remarked: "I was born for opera-buffa, Thou knowest it well!"* And indeed he is best remembered by his comic operas, in particular *Il Barbiere di Siviglia* (Rome, 1816); but in his day his serious operas also enjoyed prodigious success, notably *Tancredi* (composed when he was twenty),

---

*At Vienna in 1822, Beethoven said to Rossini: "Never try to write anything but opera-buffa..... Give us plenty of *Barbers.*"

*Otello,** Mosé, La Donna del Lago, Zelmira,*
and *Semiramide* (the last opera Rossini wrote in
Italy). The comic operas included *L'Italiana in
Algeri, La Cenerentola, La Gazza Ladra, Le
Comte Ory* (Paris, 1828). Rossini's Italian
operas were composed recklessly. The padding
was shameless; indeed, he was sometimes too
nonchalant even for his day, and he had not
infrequent checks in his gay career. But the
vivacity, the glitter of this music! All Europe
was captivated by it. The Italian school of singing was never more splendid. The day of the
eunuchs was over, but their remarkable art had
pointed the way to an extraordinary expansion
of the powers of the normal voice. Rossini's
music tells us in nearly every page of the virtuosity of the Italian operatic singing of the
times. The singers incited him; he in his turn
made ever greater demands. The vocal art, formerly exquisite, became gorgeous under Rossini,
Meyerbeer and Verdi. Rossini was furiously im-
pulsive, was audaciously witty, was a scandal
and a European delight. Compared with
Mozart's, his comic-opera style was coarse, and
Hegel was very properly ashamed of himself
when he said: "I have heard the *Barber* three

* A happy ending for Desdemona was provided
to meet the wishes of the Neapolitan public.

times in the last few days. My taste must be terribly depraved, for I like Rossini's Figaro a hundred times better than Mozart's." But still Rossini's madcap music is something the world is fortunate to possess.

For the Germans he was a "corruptor"; in Italy he was held a reformer, mainly on the grounds of his accompanied recitative, some unconventionality in orchestration (though the orchestra remained strictly subsidiary), and his practice of writing out the decorations of the melodic line (thereby limiting the improvisations of the singers). His essential reform, however, was derived from the animation of his character. He made a blaze just when the Germans were going in for rich gloom. *Tell,* perhaps, was a theme he had better have left to them. He had to labour over this opera — which was therefore his last. It is an enormous work, as long as *Die Meistersinger.* The Italian composer tackled a German subject in a French text: an impossible task; but Rossini cannot fairly be blamed for failing in 1829 to appreciate the causes of its impossibility (the break-up of the old Europeanism, the new separatist consciousness of the peoples, the splitting of music, like Latin in the Dark Ages, into independent dialects). So clever a man as Spontini thought (in the same year as *Tell*) that it was open to him, as a member of the European musical profession, to compose a German opera, *Agnes von Hohenstaufen,* when, as we can see now, he might almost as well have tried to write German poetry; and Meyerbeer, likewise a clever man, went on for more than thirty years after *Tell* composing operas in what may be called the imperial manner, not realizing that he was behind the times (or at least not so much ahead of the times as the artist needs to be), and that the old musical empire was disintegrating. Rossini was the soul of the European gaiety of the post-Napoleonic peace. After the July revolution he may have perceived that — although it was open to him to share Meyerbeer's ephemeral successes for a generation — his day was really over. The coming day was that of the nationalists, German Wagner and Italian Verdi. If, on the one hand, Rossini felt the hollowness of success in France (where "imperial" music lasted longest, down to 1870), on the other hand he had no stomach for a share in the glory of the new, the heroic Verdian age in Italy, as was shown (if the silence of his Muse was not enough) by his absurd flight from Bologna in the alarums of '48.

Meyerbeer's principal operas were produced

in Paris, where under the July monarchy and
throughout the Second Empire the scene enjoyed great social prestige and the spectacle and
the appointments were splendid. These works,
once the talk of Europe, but now, for all their
qualities, desuete, were: *Robert le Diable*
(1831), *Les Huguenots* (1836), *Le Prophète*
(1849), and the posthumous *Africaine* (1865).
Meyerbeer's education was international and not
less so his career. The defects in his style,
compared with such an earlier cosmopolitan
composer as Gluck, indicate the altered character of essential music in the new century. The
story of the shaping of each of his operas shows
him as astonishingly complaisant towards dubi-
ous friends of musical art. The various managers
of the Paris opera seem to have regarded music
as a mere accessory to their sumptuous shows;
managers, librettists, singers and dancers all had
a say in the form Meyerbeer's music took. This
remarkable man, a man of undoubted genius,
appears to have lacked inner convictions; he
abounded in ideas but had no leading idea. It
comes to this, that the effect of Meyerbeer's
operas is disconcertingly patchy.* *Les Huguenots,* his masterpiece, contains capital pages,

* Wagner said of them that they were effects
without causes.

notably the exciting "consecration of the daggers" in the fourth act. But the enormously long opera is a piecemeal composition, not a structure. The more or less historical subjects of the Meyerbeer operas — the victims of St. Bartholomew's eve, John of Leyden, and Vasco da Gama — would have been hard to fit with a consistent music by anyone; and Meyerbeer was the last man to think of consistency. Thus he set Marguerite de Valois to sing a typical coloratura soprano's song, making at once an effect of a concert in fancy dress. It is not that sixteenth-century characters in opera must necessarily sing sixteenth-century music; but the conventionality of Marguerite's song quarrels with the real matter of *Les Huguenots,* a matter that is always being pushed aside for the sake of decorations. The oddity of the composer's taste is seen in the one "historical" effect in the opera: when, at the end, the martyrs of the Paris massacre of 1572 are set to sing Luther's hymn! The Meyerbeer operas are bazaars, jumbled with goods, now valuable, now pinchbeck. He never again had a subject as good as *Les Huguenots.* He worked at *L'Africaine* for twenty years apparently without grasping its real subject. The central character is Vasco da Gama, who loves two women, one with passionate love, the other

with grateful love because she ministers to the
ambition in him, which is stronger than any
love. But Meyerbeer's Vasco is simply not char-
acterized. The self-sacrificing African Queen
might have been the central character; but, as it
is, a mass of operatic furniture stands in the way
of our clear view of her. In his day Meyerbeer's
operas excited all the capitals of Europe. They
were execrated by some of the stricter musicians
(Schumann, Chopin, Wagner) but not by any
means all. His vogue is in some measure to be
explained by the chances of exhibition he afforded to the greatest singers, in an age of vocal
virtuosity.* Meyerbeer's shortcomings and a
certain shoddiness that went with his invention
and colour have meant a great loss; the full
achievement that should have been his is wanted
— the achievement of a magnificent, entertain-
ing and sociable art, to balance or to relieve
Wagner's tyrannical solemnity.

Of the operas composed under Meyerbeer's
influence in Louis Philippe's reign, one survives,
likewise the work of a Jewish musician: *La Juive*
(1835), by Elie Halévy (1799-1862). Scribe's
libretto had been refused by Rossini. The opera

* In 1894 *Les Huguenots* was sung by Nordica,
Scalchi, Melba, Jean and Édouard de Reszke, Plan-
çon and Maurel.

(on a ghastly story of a persecution of Jews at Constanz in the fifteenth century) is no great masterpiece, but the motive wrung from the composer an expression of some consistency, though Halévy had less than Meyerbeer's brilliance and resources. *La Juive* has owed not a little to a striking part, that of the patriarchal Eleazar, exceptionally written for a robust tenor.

The musician who might, with fortune's aid, have illuminated the French lyric stage of his time — a busy stage that lacked a great musician — was the greatest of French musicians, the frustrated Hector Berlioz (1803-1869). Berlioz might write symphonies and masses, but a spectacle was always in his mind's eye. He was a dramatic musician who rebelled at the practical restrictions and discipline of opera — as also at the intercourse, the business, the nervous wear and tear of the opera-house. "Les théâtres," he exclaimed, "sont les mauvais lieux de la musique."* He had not patience enough for the problem, he was too proud of his romantic independence.** At the same time the strength of

* "Music that goes to the opera-house goes to the stews."

** "Berlioz's misery was due to his capacity for inventing sufferings for himself and to his craving for impossibilities. He harboured a wrong-headed idea,

the fortress must be recognized — the Paris
where a frivolous public could insist on having
the opera that it liked. That Paris beat Wagner.

Berlioz's operas were *Benvenuto Cellini*
(Paris, 1838), *Les Troyens* (composed 1852-
1858), and *Béatrice et Bénédict* (composed
1860, produced at Baden 1862). The first had
its origins in Berlioz's Roman impressions,
formed when he was a scholar at the Villa
Medici. The opera was composed in 1835-1836,
reached the stage only after heart-breaking
vicissitudes, was sung four times, then was
dropped and was not seen again in Paris for
seventy-four years. Berlioz conducted the work
in London (Drury Lane) in 1853, Liszt at Weimar in 1855 and Bülow at Hannover in 1879.
Cellini contained proofs of genius in plenty,
notably the overture and the carnival-finale of
the second act. But the interest is all episodical.
The dramatic motives are both inadequate —
the abduction of the girl Teresa and the casting
of the Perseus — and this was something which
Paris, quick to depreciate bad theatre, could not
forgive. The fact is that Berlioz's genius fell
between two stools. His *Roméo et Juliette* sym-

one that he also did much to disseminate — namely,
that a composer had no business to take into account
material obstacles." (Saint-Saëns).

phony seems like a concert-reduction of an opera, while *Cellini* and *Les Troyens* lack a dramatic mainspring.

Les Troyens belongs to the last phase of his career, but the subject (like that of nearly every one of his larger compositions) had been planted in his mind during his enthusiastic youth. Again and again in his disillusioned middle and latter years, when his guardian angel was warning him that he was spoiling his life, — again and again he grasped at one or other of the visions of the bygone time when all things had seemed possible. As a small boy Berlioz had delighted in Virgil, and the *Aeneid* was the inspiration of this, the last of his major works. For *Les Troyens* the world is partly indebted to Liszt's Russian mistress, the Princess Caroline Sayn-Wittgenstein. That celebrated blue-stocking pressed Berlioz to undertake an opera on a classic theme, and even sketched the scenario which, under her encouragement, he himself elaborated into a libretto. By the beginning of 1857 an act and a half was composed. In May, 1858, the whole work was ready for performance, and excerpts were played at Baden. But Berlioz, even at this stage of his career, had not the entry to the Paris Opéra. His rejoicings over the failure of *Tannhäuser* (1861), which read so disagree-

ably, are to be put down to the acidity of oft-
frustrated hopes. Berlioz never heard his grand-
iose work performed in full. Carvalho of the
Théâtre Lyrique, whose offer he had accepted,
could not cope with it as a whole. The first two
acts (*La Prise de Troie*) were therefore abandoned, and the rest was produced as *Les Troyens à
Carthage*. It was not the total failure some have
made it out to have been; twenty-two performances were given, and Choudens, the publisher,
paid 15,000 francs for the score. *Les Troyens* is
now published as two operas, although as performed in Paris it is (by large excisions) reduced
to one evening's entertainment. *La Prise de
Troie* was first performed at Karlsruhe in 1890,
under Mottl. Both parts were performed at
Glasgow in 1935.

There are some today who hold *Les Troyens*
to be a supreme masterpiece.* No one can deny
the magic of its great moments. Cassandra, the
apparition of Hector's ghost, and then the
tragedy of Dido, touched the composer's imagination. Then flashed Berlioz's peculiar poetry
of sound. But, like all who have treated the
classic theme, he could not warm to Aeneas; and
when Berlioz could not warm he fell back on a

* "One of the most gigantic and convincing masterpieces of music-drama". (D. F. Tovey).

perfunctory style. We have reached a period in which Wagner is never out of mind. Wagner would never have taken up the Trojan story; all the pathos of Cassandra and Dido notwithstanding, he would have turned down a story whose hero left him cold. But if we can imagine his taking it up he would at least have disguised his boredom, for to inspiration he had learnt to add craft, a craft that could carry on the oratory of Fricka, Wotan, Gurnemanz, after the flash had faded. At the very end the old weaver, in *Parsifal,* was still spinning his yarns so cunningly that the transition from the real to the artificial is imperceptible. In the fifties Berlioz was tiring of life. He, too, had pretended fairly heavily at times, but his pretences did not last so well, himself not (or hardly) having been taken in. "I might end by having made for myself quite a pretty career," he said, "if only I could live to be 140." Well, his success in the twentieth century would have had a tart flavour for him, depending as it does on his foil — his clear colour showing up on the background of the German's forest-greens. It is a success that comes of that craving for some sort of "Mediterranean music," felt by Nietzsche and many since, after a satiation of Wagner. But Wagner does not belong to this chapter, which embraces *Les*

Troyens as being the last Gluckian opera. If the Paris theatre could not accommodate Berlioz it was to find out too late how much it stood in need of him. Hence the attempts to adapt *La Damnation de Faust* for the stage (Monte Carlo, 1893, Liverpool, 1894, Paris, 1903, Covent Garden, 1933). *Béatrice et Bénédict* is graceful but trifling.

IV

THE MODERN PERIOD

WEBER and Rossini were great men, but they were to have greater heirs. The same year saw the birth of the two giants of nineteenth-century dramatic music. Giuseppe Verdi (1813-1901) took up the much-played instrument of Italian opera; it renewed itself in his hands, sounded thrilling tones of heroism and passion, then at the end acquired new chords of deeper and more subtle expression. Richard Wagner (1813-1883) had the more elaborate task; he had practically to contrive a new instrument. For what did opera count in German music compared with the symphony? The Beethoven symphony was "the opera of the orchestra" (E. T. A. Hoffmann). For the German composer coming after Beethoven — succeeding to Beethoven — the opera instrument had to be able, if it was to be worth thinking about, to play the symphony.

Wagner was born at Leipzig just after the outbreak of the "War of Liberation" and a few months before the battle there „of the Nations."

That war marks the beginning of the new
Germany of the nineteenth century, the powerful, essential member of Europe that the old
Germany (divided, provincial, imitative in its
culture) had never been; the birth was that of
the man who was to incarnate in the world's
eyes the German soul. He was not to do it by
means of the German language which the world
declines, except under compulsion, to read; he
was naturally to do it through music (a language in which the German countries possessed
tradition, culture and achievements of genius
comparable with those of literary England), and
not through music alone, or the unmusical
world might not have fully appreciated him,
but through music in association with the
theatre.

Wagner's operas were the following:
Die Feen (composed 1833-1834, performed
Munich 1888).
Das Liebesverbot (composed 1834, perform-
ed Magdeburg 1836).
Rienzi (composed 1838-1840, performed
Dresden 1842, London 1879).
Der fliegende Holländer (composed 1840-
1841, performed Dresden 1843, London 1870).
Tannhäuser (composed 1844, performed

Dresden 1845, Paris 1861, London 1876).

Lohengrin (composed 1847-1848, performed Weimar 1850, London 1875).

*Der Ring des Nibelungen:**

Das Rheingold (composed 1853-1854, performed Munich 1869).

Die Walküre (composed 1854-1856, performed Munich 1870).

Siegfried (Act I. and part of Act II., composed 1857, composition resumed and completed 1869, performed Bayreuth 1876).

Götterdämmerung (composed 1870-1874, performed Bayreuth 1876).****

Tristan und Isolde (composed 1857-1859, performed Munich 1865, London 1882).

Die Meistersinger von Nürnberg (composed 1862-1867, performed Munich 1868, London 1882).

Parsifal (composed 1877-1878, performed Bayreuth 1822, New York 1903, London 1914).

Out of the mass of biographical matter (which must cause Wagner's Shade to envy

* The libretto was begun with Götterdämmerung (Siegfrieds Tod) in 1848. The whole libretto was printed in 1853.

** The Ring was performed in London in 1882.

Shakespeare's happier personal obscurity, for the Shade would surely be better pleased if musicology were busy, like the Baconians, in proving that *Die Meistersinger* was really composed by Ludwig II. or Bismarck, instead of giving so much attention to his extra-conjugal kisses) — out of the masses of Wagnerian biography let us pick a few facts of significance. Wagner was brought up in the world of the theatre. His father, who died too soon to know him, was a clerk who had had some kind of legal education and was devoted to the theatre and literature. His stepfather* was an actor. "My earliest memories are associated with my stepfather and through him with the theatre. My imagination was impressed not only by the spectacle, by access to the stage and to the stage wardrobe, but also by my actually taking part in the performances", (Mein Leben). His brother Albert and his sisters followed the theatrical career. The autobiography (self-complacent and disingenuous but very readable) tells of his keen literary interests as a schoolboy. The theatre and books, then, came before music into his experience. At twelve he began to have piano lessons. At fifteen he wrote a tragedy, then thought of

* Ludwig Geyer, whom some believe to have really been his father.

setting it to music, then set about acquiring the technics of composition. Soon he decided, under the influence of Beethoven's and Weber's music, to be a composer, a composer and nothing else. The force of his early decision was aided by the ease with which, in his artistic, somewhat bohemian family, he managed to obtain serious musical instruction. His adolescent mind fed on Shakespeare, Schiller and Goethe as well as on opera and symphony. At nineteen his more or less Beethovenian symphony was played at Prague and Leipzig; it gives evidence of useful musical technics. A considerable man of letters then offered him an opera text. This was declined; Wagner had his own views on what a libretto should be, and was already decided now and henceforward to write his own.

Wagner in his next stage was writing prentice operas and conducting. At Würzburg he was appointed chorus master at the theatre, and took to Marschner's music. He conducted opera at Magdeburg when twenty-one, was appointed to the Königsberg theatre two years later, and after a year to Riga. Conditions at Magdeburg were almost squalid; in the Baltic theatres they were fairly rough. What interests us is that in these young years Wagner went through the rough-and-tumble of practice. His gift from

nature was ideas, genius; but it was not developed in the void. He was, in time, to realize his
ideal theatre; the dreams of genius went to its
making, but also the experience of what an
actual theatre was. He knew himself to be the
man of destiny. He nursed his genius with the
jealousy that belongs to genius. Now, and all
along, he was unbearable to all who were not
interested in that sacred charge. He was ruthless.
All that there is to be said for him is that he
had a powerful motive in his life, a motive
which he carried unfalteringly to its issue. Wagner, as has been made out only too clearly, was
a cad in regard to his friends, his creditors,
fellow-artists, his mistresses and his Minna. But
let us remember that Wagner was a man possessed; and what possessed him is now our
possession.

While in quasi-exile at Riga he composed
Rienzi, an enormously long and sumptuous
opera, less German than Spontinian. Paris was
then the finest theatre in Europe, with most
wealth and most prestige. *Rienzi* was composed
with such requirements in the execution and
spectacle as could be fully met only on the stage
of *Tell* and *Les Huguenots.* With *Rienzi* well
on the way to completion Wagner therefore set
out on the conquest of Paris. This Napoleonic

campaign was a failure. It remains a favourite subject of speculation, what would have been the history of music if Wagner had succeeded in Paris as Lully, Gluck, Cherubini, Rossini and Meyerbeer succeeded there.

Though without knowing it, Germany wanted him. There was a land of a hundred theatres but no national theatre. It was a rich and vacant land, with *Die Zauberflöte* and Weber's operas as green shoots hinting what might grow. It wanted a powerful hand to till, and Wagner's single-handed accomplishing of the task still appears an almost incredible feat. For what was it? It was not only the fulfilment of Weber's promise and not only the application of German instrumental art to the drama; it was the giving to Germany itself, its inhabitants and its forests and hills, for the first time practically, the definition and significance of poetic thought.*

The Paris campaign, then, was futile, unless indeed the sting that Wagner's vanity received spurred him on to the predestined German way. The man of the world in him could not help delighting in the French people (although in

---

* So that when you see in spring a field of flowers in the Bavarian Alps, with snow on the mountains behind, it is not merely a piece of nature; but you say: "Good Friday in Parsifal!"

1871 he was guilty of a cheap gibe at the defeated foe); but after *Rienzi*, a hard and showy opera, the last concessions had been made and the artist in him turned completely away from them.

The Dresden period (1842-1848) saw the brilliant production of *Rienzi;* that of the less warmly welcomed *Holländer* (which had been composed in Paris on a subject borrowed from Heine); the composition and production of *Tannhäuser;* the composition of *Lohengrin*. Wagner was given a conductor's post at the Dresden opera. Fortune smiled; the composer was in an agreeable social, financial and artistic position that he might have been expected to enjoy till his death. The daimon within him, however, would not let him be.

Wagner's Dresden operas have poetic force; with all their crudities they are the work of genius, they survive; the streaks of pure poetry are rich (thus the sea in the *Holländer*, Tannhäuser's battling in the tides of passion, the radiance of Lohengrin's apparition), and when the poetry is inferior it still sums up, very pleasingly for us, the fashions of romantic sentiment. In *Lohengrin* the heroine is a goose — but charmingly dated.

The position in the 1840's was that those

operas were rather too good for Dresden — but
Wagner was only beginning. He was cramped
there and had to get away. He had accumulated
a library of German mythical and medieval lore;
the subjects of all the later operas were in his
head; but there were too many actual Germans
pressing around for him to achieve the new
poetry of Germany. The Dresden operas represent something of a compromise (though
not a conscious one) between the opera-going
burgessy and his poeticizing and idealizing
power. It was more possible to see from a distance the soul of Germany, free and fearless
(*Siegfried*, Zürich), or the lovableness of the
genial, musical, open-hearted German burgessy
(*Meistersinger*, Paris).

The insurrectionary skirmishes at Dresden in
1849 were the occasions of Wagner's departure.
Years of unrest and virtual homelessness followed. Wagner had learnt what the theatre was.
Now he cut himself off from it to work out his
reform. For five years he composed no music.
He began again with *Rheingold* (1853). In the
meantime he had hammered out his theory of
opera — with toil and sweat, so we judge by
the prose works whose torturing style contrasts
so remarkably with the limpidness and ease of
the music that was soon to come in floods. With

Wagner, music was not a closed compartment of the mind; and given the general idea he seems to have had no difficulty with the musical expression. The book of the *Ring* — which was developed backwards from Siegfried's tragedy — was the essential part of the work, on which the mere music followed naturally. The autobiography *Mein Leben* is in many respects false; but we are impressed and convinced by the accounts Wagner gives — sometimes casually, and sometimes with a kind of detached surprise — of his musical inspiration. The prelude to *Rheingold* flowed from some source beyond the will. As he improvised on a new piano, the love music of the second act of *Tristan* formed itself under his fingers. Actions and scenes, dramatic themes and motives were worked out with labour; the rest ensued.

True, the *Ring* music took more than twenty years to write. That was partly because of the tediousness of the mere task of musical penmanship. In the second act of *Siegfried* Wagner broke off: put his *Nibelung* aside for years. The thing seemed hopeless, not in point of achievement but of practical execution, since Germany was so reluctant to open its eyes to the poet's idealization of Germany. But if *Siegfried* was put aside for *Tristan und Isolde* this was not the only reason. A passionate episode at Zürich, a more or less frustrated love affair with the wife of his benefactor Wesendonck, suggested a new theme to his creative imagination.

Then there was *Die Meistersinger*. This, the composer fondly hoped, would turn out to be practicable — more accessible and assimilable than the monstrous *Ring*. It might win helpers to build the *Ring* theatre, the German opera-house. But again, this was not all. The *Ring*, being half done, was essentially done; but the *Meistersinger* was a new thing; after the myths of the race, after medieval chivalry, this was a theme of the Germany of the Renaissance and of the middle classes, and at the same time the theme was Wagner himself, the wise, genial, mature artist, and his beautiful art, with incidental satire on his grudging, stupid enemies. A new thing presenting itself was not to be refused by Wagner, now at the height of his powers; the *Ring* could wait.

Meanwhile he had tried a fall once again with Paris. *Tannhäuser* was there turned down in 1861. It did not matter; for now Germany was open to be won. The eccentric Ludwig II. of Bavaria embraced Wagner's cause in 1864. Cosima, Liszt's strong-willed daughter, left her husband Bülow for him; loved, guarded, nursed

him and fought for him as her father had
fought for him in the decade before.

Bayreuth opened in 1876, supported by the
kings and dukes of Germany. It was all this one
man's idea and achievement: a German opera-
house at last, not like any theatre of the Latin
lands, but an opera-house in the woods, whence
frivolity was banned, and where gods and monsters, heroes and sages discoursed with solemnity, all their actions being designed to allow of
a symphonic expansion in the music, while their
dark words appeared and vanished in a forest of
orchestral harmonies. It remained for Wagner
to compose *Parsifal*. This was to work out fully
and grandly — the ageing musician now purged
of passion, having had his fill of fighting
(*Ring*), love (*Tristan*) and song-making (*Meistersinger*) — a haunting motive of the roman-
ticists, the motive of redemption, one that had
come back into poetry with the revival of
medieval sentiment. Wagner had taken it over
from Goethe (Gretchen's redemption of Faust),
and had made it a regular spring of his action
(Senta's redemption of the Dutchman — which
he took over from Heine — and Elisabeth's redemption of Tannhäuser). It was so much an
element in the air that it could not be kept out
of the paganism and pessimism of the Ring,

whose chaotic ending is tranquillized and sublimated by the suggestion, however obscure and unconvincing, that Brünnhilde's love has redeemed the world. By the time of *Parsifal* Europe was fairly won to an opera that did not amuse but impressed; that was no sociable evening but a long daydream; that explored a wilderness and added a province to civilization. Wagner's life was well rounded off and, for all the little mistakes in detail, was one of nature's best works; he did fully what he had to do, and at the end he was properly apotheosized.

The form Wagner's dramatic music took was appropriate to the change of the scene of action from sociable Mediterranean cities to the forests and mountains of the thinly populated north. Formal modes of address (the aria da capo; the Recitative, Andante and Allegro; and so on) disappeared and likewise the ensemble pieces which speak of an urbane society in which different persons can talk together without quarrelling — individually and yet harmoniously, as in the Mozartian ensemble. It is rather rare, in the sublime wilderness of the *Ring,* for human beings to meet; the early and unpopulated state of the world is indicated by (and made to be held to excuse) the incestuous relations of its inhabitants. Not till the fourth evening of the

Ring, when the tribesmen come out for Siegfried's wedding, do we learn that there are more
than two or three families in the whole world.
The compensation lies in the majesty of the un-
spoilt landscape and the breadth of action per-
missible in such spaces to the few and lordly
personages. The high primitiveness of this old
German world is further indicated by the rarity
of ordinary songs in the music (in the sociable
Meistersinger it is, of course, different). Typical
Wagnerian vocal music is declamation and
arioso, melodious and rambling. Can that fill
the gigantic frame? No; but then there is the
sympathetic orchestra, which represents the
scenery, the wash of waters and beating of
winds (and indeed represents all this so well
that the contemplation of Wagner's music is
rather like that of the endlessly interesting face
of Nature), and then embodies the human passions of the plot, so that the invisible spirits of
wrath, courage, desire and so on, are more than
the living creatures whom they sway.

Wagner's masterpiece of conception, form
and execution is *Tristan und Isolde.* The theme
is the principal human experience — the embrace of man and woman. Conventions must be
allowed every artist, and the chief convention
to be allowed Wagner is the articulateness,

articulateness copious and unrestrained, of his
characters. This granted, there is no fault to be
found with Tristan, from the birth of desire in
the opening bars to the chill of its death, when
the fever has worked itself out, in the last
pages. It is beautiful to see the thing growing
— it is as beautiful as a tree. Mark's address has
sometimes been objected to. But it is necessary
for Mark to have his say and that we should
know him, too, to be a victim of the fever of
love; it had to be made quite clear that Tristan
und Isolde were suffering simply from that.
Isolde, Tristan und Isolde, Tristan — the three
acts are shapely. As always in Wagner, the
second act is not the supremely fine one; it is
in the third act (as always) that he gathers up
his strength and with incredible reserves lays us
low. To find something at which to cavil in
Tristan one can only point to excess of dynamic
marks plastered over the sailor's song at the
beginning of the first act — directions that are
inappropriate to a folk-song.

The *Ring* is, by comparison with *Tristan,* in-
coherent. Wagner tried to get so much into it
— Odin and the Bronze Age, and Schopenhauer
as well — that he ended by not being clear
about what he really wanted. The affair of the
gods — Wotan, Fricka, Loge — is matter for

satiric comedy, but forced into tragedy. Wotan is the early nineteenth-century magnate, very powerful and rather stupid, violent and weak; at home henpecked by his wife but a tyrant to his children; in the City, a fraudulent financier whose pretensions make him absurd when his scrapes come to light. At the other end of the tetralogy is the disappointing clumsiness and brutality of the dramatizing of Siegfried's treachery to Brünnhilde. Yet, after all, gibes are easy at the expense of any cosmology. It is the strength and weakness of the *Ring* that it belongs to an age when great men fearlessly set out to be complete cosmologists.

. If the *Ring* as a whole got out of hand, in parts it remains Wagner at his best, and therefore stupendous. The loves of Siegmund and Sieglinde, of Siegfried and Brünnhilde — the one couple so afflicted and tender, the other how care-free and radiant! — escape from the oppression of sick longing of *Tristan*. What mornings are in the *Ring,* what sunsets, what awful midnights! The texture of *Rheingold* is comparatively light. *Die Walküre* is the most unequal of the four scores. It has the loveliest first act, a cumbrous and sometimes arid second act, in which are, however, such miracles of music as Brünnhilde's annunciation to Siegmund. *Sieg-*

fried is weighty and has the strength to soar with it all. Nothing shows better than the third act how triumphantly Wagner could rise when the call was highest. In the flushing dawn Brünnhilde loves and is beloved; to that everything before was the ascent, and thence everything after descends. The sinister harmonies of the Tarnhelm cast a spell over the blind world of the *Götterdämmerung*. Waltraute's hopeless appeal for the salvation of the god of gods spreads fear. Wotan in despair, unseen, is terrible at last. Nothing has become Siegfried like his death. Doomed, he at last succeeds in moving us; dead, and when the great dirge floods the tragic valley, he is a hero indeed. So to the end — a drowned world and heaven a burnt-out fire.

Die Meistersinger pours out its tunefulness for some five hours. A burgher offers to give away his daughter for a good song; luckily the best composer, who is self-taught, is young, handsome and a gentleman, while his only rival is grotesque, middle-class and, although a repository of all the rules, no composer at all.* A

* The books of *Meistersinger* and *Lohengrin* were thought out at the same time, in 1845, just before the production of *Tannhäuser*. Wagner's starting-point was not Walther and Eva, but the Sachs-Beckmesser scene in the second act.

slender subject, one might have said, fit for the lightest of comic operas. And Wagner was never known to have a light hand; the nearest he got to humour was a mood of boisterously high spirits. *Die Meistersinger* nonetheless turned out to be one of the world's wonders. How he enriched the theme, how he loaded the rifts with gold — that is as admirable as the newness of this music, so Wagnerian and yet so far both from the heroic strains of the *Ring* and the fever of *Tristan*. Such richness meant heaviness; *Meistersinger* is a prodigious weight. The listener is loaded down with the gift of Wagner's more than life-size treatment of his good Nurembergers. Was there nothing for it but that they should be as large as Valhallans? Walther is arrested to gaze at Eva (in the third act) with a *Blick* as long as that of the drugged Tristan, for the sake of the expansion of ravishing orchestral music. Beckmesser's roasting is nothing less than brutal — and is all one with the piece. Yes; there is brutality in the strength of the piece, and sentimentality in its sweetness and geniality. The Nuremberg crowd puts its finger on the right song at the end; well, it was made easy for them.

Parsifal was preserved for thirty years as the particular and unshared property of the Bayreuth

theatre whither, consequently, all Europe had
to repair in pilgrimage. *Parsifal* was obscure;
and while this may have been because there was
that in its content which was too deep for reason,
it may in part have been the old master's theatrical craft. A representation of the Eucharist
would not have been acceptable in the Latin
theatre. Wagner, in his new German theatre,
enjoyed something of the liberty of the pioneer.
The compensation for the enormous labour of
tilling the wilderness was that he could put into
it what he liked, all he had. For his last subject,
in the beautiful autumn of his art, nothing could
be too solemn or highly serene. He had had in
his mind, ever since Dresden days, a *Jesus of
Nazareth* in five acts; and the story of *Parsifal*
had been in his mind since the time of *Lohengrin* and had actually been worked at in the
1850's. Those themes matured in the ageing
Wagner, now slightly world-weary and inclined
to peaceful renunciation. *Parsifal* is a marvellous swan-song. There are times when the music
languishes with the action; we may not believe
that Gurnemanz tells the whole truth of things.
The young Wagner would have given more
substance to these Visigothic warrior-monks in
their conflict with the Paynim. But the old
magician was certain of his spells. Renunciation

was his theme, but the musician and the man of
the theatre renounced only to acquire. He grasped at the chanting in the temple, and the incense
and the painted glass were rendered by a glow-
ing orchestra. Wagner brought his chromatic
style in *Parsifal* to a new melting sweetness. The
choral ballet of the odalisques in the scene in
the renegade Klingsor's harem is bewitching
music; but the heart of the *Parsifal* music is the
stretch of orchestral song in the third act, the
scene of the wearied Parsifal's return, music
ineffably tender, wistful and serene. This was
Wagner's Nunc Dimittis.

*　　*　　*　　*

Although the names *Zauberflöte,* Weber,
Wagner, and, to include contemporaries, Strauss
sum up German opera as generally known, there
are others. Weber's and Wagner's genius eclipsed two rather noteworthy opera composers —
Louis Spohr (1784-1859) and H. A. Marschner
(1795-1861). Spohr composed, along with
masses of chamber music and symphonies, ten
operas, including *Faust* (1813), *Jessonda* (1822)
and *Die Kreuzfahrer* (1844). At Cassel he
championed Wagner's works in the days of
adversity. Wagner on his part found *Jessonda*

"not without sublimity." Marschner was a minor follower of Weber's; his operas were numerous; Germans still remember *Hans Heiling* (1833).

Wagner's more eminent contemporaries did not shine in opera. Schumann was very desirous of overthrowing the Italian hegemony. In 1847-1849 he composed *Genoveva,* which was produced at Leipzig in 1850, and whose overture survives. This opera is the equivalent of the closet dramas of our Victorian poets — the work of an artist who desired to improve the theatre without coming into too close contact with it. Wagner's hints at the faults in the libretto were not taken kindly. For Schumann Wagner "is not a good musician; he has no understanding of form or euphony" (1853). *Genoveva* is good music, euphonious, but the work suffers from a mortal sameness; text and score alike present no relief. Mendelssohn's comic opera *Die Hochzeit des Camacho* (Berlin, 1827) was composed when he was sixteen. He died leaving *Lorelei* unfinished; the fragments were written in a superannuated style. Brahms never wrote for the stage. The cantata *Rinaldo* hints at what his operatic manner might have been; it leaves us with no regrets for his abstention. *Der Barbier von Bagdad* (Weimar, 1858), by Peter Cornelius, a member of the Liszt-Wagner party, and

Goetz's *Der Widerspenstigen Zähmung* (1874)
are mid-nineteenth-century German operas that
are remembered. The one Wagnerian masterpiece not by Wagner was Engelbert Humper-
dinck's *Hänsel und Gretel* (Weimar, 1893). In
this engaging score Wagnerian harmonies and
orchestral colouring are applied to popular German tunes and a children's fairy tale.

*   *   *   *

Let us now go south again, over the Alps.
There, throughout Wagner's career, another
career had been developing: Giuseppe Verdi's.
But first (for our chapter titles are for conveni-
ence and mark no very real divisions) there are
two of the best of the Rossinians to be mentioned: Vincenzo Bellini (1801-1835) and Gaetano
Donizetti (1797-1848). Bellini's principal
operas were *La Sonnambula* (1831), *Norma*
(1831) and *I Puritani* (1835). The first is an
idyll of the Swiss mountains, the second a tragic
drama of the Gaul of the Druids, the third a
romantic drama of Roundheads and Cavaliers.
Bellini's talent, an exquisite talent, had not all
the variety that such a range of subjects might
suggest. His peculiar gift was a fount of elegant
melody. His range was limited; it was common

for his magic to depart when the movement
changed from andante to allegro. The tenderness of Bellini's expression was peculiarly his
own.

Donizetti composed in thirty years some
seventy operas, often at the rate of four a year,
grand dramas and comic operas alike, not to
speak of his drawing-room ballads and church
music. He began as an imitator of Rossini. *Anna
Bolena* (Milan, 1830) revealed a personal talent.
The gay comic opera *L'Elisir d'Amore* was one
of four operas produced in 1832. *Lucia di Lam-
mermoor* (Naples, 1835) was one of many subjects somewhat lightly adopted from British
history or romance. This work is still sung. Most
of Donizetti's serious operas, however, are forgotten, unless a graceful song or two floats to
the surface; but the comic operas, such as *La
Fille du Régiment* (Paris, 1840) or *Don Pasqu-
ale,* which was written in eleven days for Paris
in 1843, remain captivating. The gay and facile
composer was the darling of all Europe. He died
of general paralysis, insane.

Verdi's operas were the following:

THE EARLY OPERAS

Oberto (Milan, 1839); *Un giorno di Regno,*

or *Il finto Stanislao* (Milan, 1841); *Nabucco*
(Milan, 1842, Vienna, 1843, Paris, 1845);
I Lombardi (Milan, 1843; revised, 1847; as
Jérusalem, Paris, 1847); *Ernani* (Venice, 1844,
London, 1845); *I Due Foscari* (Rome, 1844);
Giovanna d'Arco (Milan, 1845, Paris, 1868);
Alzira (Naples, 1845); *Attila* (Venice, 1846);
Macbeth (Florence, 1847, revised for Paris,
1865); *I Masnadieri* (London, 1847, Paris,
1870); *Il Corsaro* (Trieste, 1848); *La Battaglia
di Legnamo* (Rome, 1849); *Luisa Miller* (Naples,
1849, Paris, 1852); *Stiffelio* (Trieste, 1850;
revised as *Aroldo,* Rimini, 1857).

THE MIDDLE OPERAS

Rigoletto (Venice, 1851, London, 1853, Paris,
1857); *Il Trovatore* (Rome, 1853, Paris, 1854,
London, 1855); *La Traviata* (Venice, 1853,
London, 1856, Paris, 1856); *Les Vêpres Sici-
liennes* (Paris, 1855; as *Giovanna di Guzman,*
Milan, 1856, *I Vespri Siciliani,* London, 1859);
Simone Boccanegra (Venice, 1857; revised,
Milan, 1881); *Un Ballo in Maschera* (Rome,
1859, London and Paris, 1861); *La Forza del
Destino* (St. Petersburg, 1862, London, 1867;
revised for Milan, 1869, Paris, 1876); *Don*

Carlos (Paris, 1867; revised, 1883); *Aida* (Cairo, 1871, Milan, 1872, London and Paris, 1876).

THE LAST OPERAS

Otello (Milan, 1887, London, 1889, Paris, 1894); *Falstaff* (Milan, 1893, London and Paris, 1894).

The greatest of modern Italian composers was formerly underrated by English criticism; indeed, the treatment he gets in such a work as Parry's *Art of Music* amounts to no consideration at all. Stanford was an exception; and his appreciation of the masterpieces of Verdi's last period has had a certain influence upon English opinion. But Parry dismissed Verdi, or at least the earlier Verdi, as a mere writer of popular tunes.

Falstaff may well attract even those who can find the least possible response to the hasty, fiery music of the younger Verdi; but the composer's essential element is to be found in the earlier operas. Verdi was careless in respect to the details of workmanship of which his public was not likely to take much notice — Verdi emphasized the musical means of appealing to his audience — that is the ground of Parry's disparagement. It is the criticism of the peace-loving and imperturbable man who has no thought of a state in which the pulse of the artist and his public alike is beating quicker than the normal — in which art is less thought than deed and an operatic finale may be the bridge to an insurrectionary fusillade. There is no dissociating the artist and his life; or Verdi's music and the passions of the Risorgimento. Its love-songs are as fierce and hasty as a soldier's on leave. Martial sounds are never far away; and there is little time and less need for the introspective kind of melancholy when duty points to action.

The spirit of Verdi's music was from the first high-hearted and stirring. To that the character of the man — simple, strong and devoted — contributed essentially, of course; and so also did the spirit of the times and the patriotic call. Even in his treatment of a banal Parisian theme — *La Traviata* — something characteristically noble-hearted stands out; the call to the son to sacrifice his private luxury is in Verdi more than a family affair, it becomes a call from the country to its children for selfsacrifice. The courtesan herself is noble in urging her lover to take the path of duty.

If in the love-songs the suitor is often as brusque as a soldier, the patriotic songs are full of tenderness, as witness, "O, tu Palermo" in *I Vespri Siciliani,* "Dagl' immortali vertici" in *Attila,* and, above all, "O cieli azzurri" in *Aida.* The prayers in Verdi's operas have the solemn and manly character of prayers before battle (thus "Tu sul labbro" in *Nabucco*). The songs of hate and vengeance are characteristically conscious of a just cause, the revolutionary's cause against the tyrant (this is the spring of Iago's "Credo" in *Otello*) — or else they have the tragic pathos of lament over a traitor to the cause of righteousness (thus "Eri tu" in the *Ballo in Maschera*). Mazzini's faith, Garibaldi's bravery, the spirit of '48 vibrate for us still in this music. The preparation for Verdi is not Wagnerian theory but a reading of Trevelyan. That will provide a background to his whole work, so that even a love-song like "Celeste Aida" will seem (like certain of Swinburne's revolutionary poems, which use the language of amorous address) to derive its high tone from the inspiration not of mortal woman but of the patriot's or political visionary's ideal State.

Verdi was born in the lowliest circumstances, the son of a village innkeeper. He was taught by the church organist. While still a boy he found a patron in Antonio Barezzi, a distiller of Busseto, whose daughter he was later to marry. At eighteen Verdi was refused admission to the Milan Conservatory. He studied for two years with the Milanese composer Lavigna. Encouragement was not lacking for the young Verdi, notably from the impresario Merelli. The name of the unsuccessful comic opera, *Un giorno di regno,* is remembered because of the terrible circumstances of its composition: within a few weeks first an infant son, then a daughter, and then the young musician's wife died. In the first performance of *Nabucco,* Verdi's first true success, took part the singer Giuseppa Strepponi, who became his mistress and whom eventually he married. The *Lombardi* made him a popular hero. Soon *Nabucco* won international fame. *Ernani* came out and had a wild success. Other operas of the early period were less fortunate — usually owing to some literary flimsiness or fault. *Stiffelio* was the last failure. After the 1840's Verdi was a great European figure, the composer to whom both London and Paris turned for music to enhance international exhibitions.

Verdi's lot was easy — so far as the word can ever be applied to the creative artist's life of travail, which makes the lot of woodman, smith or miner seem easy indeed! His only external troubles came from the pettifogging and nervous censors in the different states of disunited Italy. All the capitals of Europe paid him homage; only the German intelligentsia sulked. *La Forza del Destino* was written for St. Petersburg, *Don Carlos* for the Paris exhibition of 1867, and *Aida* for the opening of Ismail Pasha's opera-house at Cairo. In the 1880's Verdi was the lion of Italy. The production of *Otello,* then that of *Falstaff,* were European events. In the last years he composed a few pages of sacred music. The tremendous Requiem had come long before, soon after *Aida.* Worn, unclouded in intellect, and sad as often are the very old when so unclouded, Verdi died in his eighty-eighth year at the villa of Sant' Agata, which he had built on the site of his father's humble house. His second wife had died three years before. Most of his fortune was left to found an almshouse for musicians at Milan.

That Wagner and Verdi should have flourished in the same continent and century and should both have been apotheosized in the same art is a sign of the richness of modern opera. The Italian was and remained to the end of his days a shrewd and sturdy peasant, jealous of his independence, little given to society, reserved in speech and pen. About the German there was something incorrigibly bohemian; he was restless, glib, given to deceit (including self-deceit), given to show. Both were indomitable, but in different ways. Wagner fought with violent gestures and groans; Verdi with doggedness. And we do not know which to admire the more — Wagner for making after all the best of himself and overcoming the hostility of the world, or Verdi for putting up a victorious fight for the best of himself against the world's adulation.

It is curious how Wagner had chances that Verdi had not. By comparison with the musical life of Wagner's Leipzig and with his education under such a man as Weinlig Verdi's Milan and Lavigna were poor indeed. The young Verdi had nothing of the young Wagner's bookish enthusiasm. At fifty Verdi was still liable to take up texts whose faults Wagner at twenty would have ridiculed. A bad libretto is not to be regarded simply as the composer's bad luck. "Do you suppose," asked Weber, "that any proper composer will allow a libretto to be put into his hand like an apple?" A faulty libretto is the composer's fault. Verdi's faults of judgment were so numerous, the shortcomings of his culture such that it is all the more marvellous what came at last. The peasant was uncouth, he was also an obstinate cultivator. The middle-period operas were composed mostly on texts by F. M. Piave, who worked under Verdi's suggestion, with results neither too bad nor too good. If there is much to be said for his *Rigoletto* and *Traviata* — thanks to Hugo and to the younger Dumas — there is too little merit in Piave's *Boccanegra* and *La Forza*.

Ernani (which was the first of the Piave operas) represents the young Verdi at his best. It scores by driving force, not subtlety. No one stops to think — all is passion — and this seemed natural to Verdi, who by that token was the predestined and incomparable musician of *Otello*. We cannot picture a Wagnerian Othello. Hugo was raided for *Ernani* (as later for *Rigoletto*), Schiller for *I Masnadieri* and *Luisa Miller,* as, much later, for *Don Carlos. Luisa Miller* contains an exceptional pensive quality which sends the mind back to Bellini.

All the operas of the 1840's were eclipsed by the splendid three that came soon, *Rigoletto, Trovatore, Traviata.* The first is most remarkable for its variety, the second for its fieriness, the third for grace and pathos. It argues a certain ingenuousness in Verdi's character that he should have taken to these themes, especially to the out-and-out horrors of the first two. No matter; in his simplicity he was great. It was a kind of heroic simplicity, untouchable by mockery. The principal shortcoming of *Trovatore* is, after all, one of a mere practical nature which improved stage technics could remedy. The opera is in eight different scenes; this usually means seven long intervals and a dissipation of interest in consequence. The intrinsic fault is the abruptness of the climax in the terrible final scene. The libretto of *Il Trovatore* has been too much disparaged. It is a complicated drama of warring passions perceived only in a series of broken glimpses. The story of the Troubadour is shown in a series of flashes, separated by clouds of darkness. Verdi would not have been true to his characters if he had sought to explain them — characters who, burning life recklessly, hadn't it in their natures to stop to explain it to themselves. The haste of these passions and the mystery of a life inflamed by one passion — love or lust, hate or sacred revenge — and for the rest in darkness, make the poetry of *Il Trovatore* as of the related *Forza del Destino*. It is a poetry which moves us to hardly any pity, but excites and exhilarates us by contact with lives more proud and violent than our own.

Verdi's mature manner begins to show in *Un*

ballo in maschera. The old vehemence was a little toned down, and in compensation came an enriched harmonic and orchestral interest. The music points to *Aida. Don Carlos,* a very long opera — too long, like others that Verdi wrote for Paris and other foreign scenes, in which against his better judgment he went to Meyerbeerian lengths — showed more signs of his increasing control and variety. This fine work has hardly ever been given its due. *Aida,* on the other hand, enjoyed from the first an unbroken triumph. The subject was suggested by Racine's *Bajazet.* The details of the Egyptian setting were due to the French Egyptologist Mariette. Camille du Locle wrote out the drama under Verdi's eye; Ghislanzoni put it into Italian verse. In *Aida* is the climax of many generations of operatic pomp and grandeur; properly executed, it is the most splendid and imposing spectacle of the European stage. As a singer's opera it is a classic. This music sets down for all time what the greatest master demanded from Italian singing at its best period. In *Aida* Verdi's hand never faltered; through four long acts his invention flowed in a full stream.

He was nearly sixty; it looked as though he had touched his zenith. Finer work was, however, still to come. For all the passion in *Aida* the personages were types rather than characters. Shakespeare lent Verdi a group of incomparable characters for his greatest masterpiece, *Otello*. And now there befell the old musician the rarest fortune: he gained as good a collaborator as musician ever had — Arrigo Boito (1842-1918). Boito, half Italian, half Polish, was himself a good musician but a better poet. He was a man of European culture. He drew on Goethe's *Faust* for his own opera *Mefistofele* (1868, revived 1875). He translated *Tristan*. As composer Boito lacked technical facility and vital impulse. He worked for half a century over *Nerone* (produced 1924). He lives in *Otello* and *Falstaff*. Verdi had written *Rigoletto* in six weeks; he spent some six years thinking over *Otello*. The opera, the greatest work of the Italian lyric theatre, came out on the stage that had seen his *Oberto* forty-eight years before. In *Otello* Verdi developed but he never broke with his past. It is a work of maturity, not of old age. The characteristic passionateness is there, but condensed and more than formerly refined in expression. The music has a new continuity;*

* Already in 1867 conservative French critiscism had accused Verdi of "anarchism" for his modifacations of regular forms, and *Don Carlos* was called a "mélopée interminable."

it closely embraces the subject in all the situations. In exchange for "Now, for ever farewell the tranquil mind" and "Now, by yond marble heaven" Verdi gives Othello regular, thoroughgoing Verdi-isms, which are taken, as they are given, utterly naturally and utterly appropriately. And it is impossible to pass on without a word for Desdemona's music. Verdi must have been wrapped up heart and soul in Shakespeare's Desdemona, to find strains for her so right and true.

*　　　*　　　*　　　*

In his eightieth year Verdi produced his third Shakespearian opera, *Falstaff*.* It was a completely new thing: an Italian comic opera, yet not facile but packed with significant music. The sap in Verdi's art, the riches of his soil! There were young men about in the 1890's, but no one so youthful or original as he. Verdi's roots were always going deeper, his mind ever growing. Boito gave him an admirable libretto. The Italian intrigue which Shakespeare in no very happy hour imposed upon Falstaff thus returned home. Verdi made it so much his own, match-

---

* The first was *Macbeth*. At different times in his life he thought much of a *Lear*.

ing every point with laughing, bustling, piquant music, and delicious strains to the young loves of Fenton and Anne Page, that the whole might well be taken to have been, like *Die Meistersinger,* the thought of one mind.

The French school meanwhile had had no such great man as Wagner or Verdi. Opera, however, was unceasingly cultivated and was adorned by men of talent. Down to the Second Empire, and even after, the French operatic situation was dominated by the fact of the existence of an opera-going public, keen and assiduous but not specifically musical, who went for the general theatrical show, in which music was expected to play a conventional part. Berlioz (whose failure with *Cellini* makes 1838 a date of disaster) and Wagner, we have seen, did not succeed with this public, who liked only what they were used to and insisted on having what they liked. Among the composers who agreed to their condition not without grace was Ambroise Thomas (1811-1896), who, with true Second Empire light-heartedness, raided Shakespeare and Goethe and gave both Hamlet and Mignon happy endings.* Charles Gounod

---

* *Mignon,* 1866 (performed 100 times in six months; 1,000th performance, Opéra Comique, 1894). *Hamlet,* 1868. Thomas's *Songe d'une nuit d'été*

(1818-1893) also went to Goethe (*Faust,* 1859) and Shakespeare (*Roméo et Juliette,* 1867); he gave Gretchen and Juliet waltz-songs to sing for Mme. Carvalho's sake. Both composers had a certain elegance and charm, especially Gounod, whose *Faust* has been one of the most popular of operas. Curious and characteristic is the Introduction to that work: a sombre, effective fugato is begun, is well written for a few bars, then is suddenly abandoned; we hear the composer saying: "But this will never do for them!" The lightly sensuous music of the Garden Scene is not unjustly celebrated; and some of the more brilliant music of the opera is clever. The style, as always with Gounod, vacillates. Faust was at first an opera with spoken dialogue; the recitative was written a year later. Paris saw the 1,500the performance in 1912. Most of Gounod's operas are now forgotten. *Roméo,* a poor piece of work for a man of such talent, is not without some characteristic sweetness. Ernest Reyer (1823-1909), a disciple of Berlioz and, through him, of Gluck, wrote *Sigurd* (Brussels, 1884) another rendering of Götterdämmerung which in France was for a time more acceptable

(Midsummer Night's Dream) (1850) introduced Falstaff and also a love-affair between Shakespeare and Queen Elizabeth.

than Wagner's. Georges Bizet (1838-1875)
composed in 1872 charming incidental music
for Daudet's *Arlésienne,* which Reyer, an excellent critic, at once praised for its "delicate harmonies, the elegant outline of the phrases and
pretty details in the scoring." In 1875 came
*Carmen** — in March; and in June Bizet's
death. The celebrated opera owes much to
Mérimée's story. But Bizet had a dazzling talent;
his music still burns with a clear flame. Less
charming but otherwise full of typical French
qualities was Saint-Saëns (1835-1921), who like
Bizet was a brilliant pianist. It is curious that his
most successful opera, *Samson et Dalila* (a
stately if not a vital composition) should for
years have been excluded from the Paris stage;
Weimar saw *Samson* in 1877, Paris in 1892.
The typical opera composer of the Third Re-
public was Jules Massenet (1842-1912). He
wrote some thirty operas, including *Hérodiade*
(1881), *Manon* (1884), *Werther* (1892) and
Thaïs (1894). Massenet was Gounod's heir. His
lyre had few strings, but he played on them very
prettily, if for too long. Massenet's operas were
all virtually an expansion of a drawing-room
song; but his drawing-room was no vulgar one,

* London, in Italian, 1878; in English, 1879; in
French, 1886.

DEBUSSY   115

his taste was delicate — in his own circle he was
a charmer. *Manon,* his masterpiece, best survives
exportation.

Massenet's most remarkable pupil was Claude
Debussy (1862-1918) who showed traces of his
master's influence in his early works but none
in his only opera *Pelléas et Mélisande* (1902).
Debussy was a pianist, a poet, a recluse; a man
of almost excessive sensibility, shy, proud, fast-
idious to the last degree. Those characteristics
are seen in his singular opera, the text of which
is a romantic play by Maeterlinck, extremely
mannered, wan and almost pulseless. Debussy
set the unhappy murmurings of the personages
of the tale in a kind of *stile rappresentativo,* like
the early Italians. In the background his orchestra rendered the faint rustling and sighing
of Maeterlinck's forest. *Pelléas* begins by charming the ear with its rare, silvery-grey sound; it
goes on to a wearisome monotony; but then,
later still, the listener is won again, when the
adolescent lovers, with no outcries, almost
dumbly indeed, drift to their doom to a music
that maintains its delicately aloof style to the
last, truly heroically. The vein was effete. Even
Debussy seems to have felt *Pelléas* to be a dead
end, for though for ten years he talked of a
Tristan that was to set off an utterance of finely

bred, chivalric lovers against the bellowings of Bayreuth, nothing came of it.

*　　　*　　　*　　　*

Meanwhile Verdi and Wagner both had successors of a sort to make Debussy shudder. The principal post-Verdians were three: Leoncavallo (1858-1919), Puccini (1858-1924), Mascagni (1863-1945). The last set the Tiber on fire in 1890 with *Cavalleria Rusticana;* the first emulated and rather surpassed him with *I Pagliacci* (1892). Both were soon to be practically eclipsed by the second of the trio, the most popular opera composer, one may say the only regularly popular one, of latter days. Leoncavallo and Mascagni never in their later operas quite hit the mark, but Puccini scored a series of successes. *Cavalleria* and *Pagliacci* were terse, bloody dramas of meridional peasant life. The crudities are formidable, and they are not the crudities of early Verdi — the heroic age is gone. Leoncavallo's is the superior work, but the stroke of repeating a four-bar strain (in the chorus "Evviva!"), simply shifted up a semitone without modulation, is perhaps the most vulgar thing in music. The new police-court operas had the merit of being alive. The strength of the

composers was this, that they were heart and
soul interested, and so were the audiences. Puccini was perfectly sincere in his sentimentality
(*Bohème* and *Butterfly*) and brutal sensational-
ism (*Tosca*). He never chose a fine theme, but
he was an artist; his letters should be read to
see his hard, honourable search for the themes
that for him were right.* Puccini's principal
operas were *Manon Lescaut* (1893), *La Bohème*
(1896), *Tosca* (1900), *Madama Butterfly*
(1904), *La Fanciulla del West* (1910), *Gianni
Schicchi (1918),* and the posthumous *Turandot*
(1926). The second and sixth of these are his
masterpieces; both, but the latter particularly,
owe much to *Falstaff.* Puccinian opera is terse;
it begins, unlike previous opera, at half-past
eight.** The technics are masterly — the sharp,
direct strokes of action, then the brief but intense lyrical expatiations. *Turandot* fails because
the central figure, the enigmatical and cold
princess, gave Puccini no hold. He needed warm

---

* We see him saddled with a pompous, sham-
idealistic "Hymn to Latin Art," given to Cavaradossi
at the beginning of the third act of *Tosca,* at last rejecting it, and insisting on his hero's getting the
lament that helped to make the fortune of the opera.

** *Rigoletto* was an exceptionally short opera for
its period.

blood at the heart of the action. He prepared
for the big scene well with an agitated prelude
(the first act); then staved off the failure with
a vivacious harlequinade, which is another off-
shoot from *Falstaff;* but the big scene when it
comes is null. The whole theme is rather repel-
lent. When the lovers, having waded through
blood, were to begin (almost before the wails
of the victims had ceased) to celebrate their
happiness in a duet, Puccini's pen dropped. The
unfinished act was given an ending by Franco
Alfano. Other operas of the time were Gior-
dano's *Andrea Chénier* (1896) and *Fedora*
(1898), Alfano's *Resurrezione* (1904) and
Wolf-Ferrari's *Giojelli della Madonna* (1911).
If all this represents a falling-off from Verdi it
is, nonetheless, a continuation, a popular art.
Wolf-Ferrari's *Giojelli* was perhaps only clever
humbug; but the rest of the school both did
their best and naturally breathed the air of the
upper galleries. After Puccini's death the composers of Italian operas were refined musicians,
e.g. Pizzetti and Malipiero, who had no more
contact with the masses than corresponding
composers in other countries; and the masses
went to the cinema.

Richard Strauss (b. 1864), the musician of
Wilhelm II.'s Germany, makes Wagner appear

wonderfully pure and elevated. Strauss's first operas were, indeed, exercises in Wagner's manner: *Guntram* (1894) and the rather Nurembergish *Feuersnot* (1901). Later his music became an orgy of neo-baroque. His operas include *Salomé* (1909), *Elektra* (1909), *Der Rosenkavalier* (1911), *Ariadne auf Naxos* (1912). *Die Frau ohne Schatten* (1919), *Die Aegyptische Helena* (1928), *Arabella* (1933), *Die Schweigsame Frau* (1935), *Friedenstag* (1938). The third of these is his masterpiece. *Salomé* and *Elektra* are Straussian tone-poems with the addition of a scenic illustration. The voices on the stage are used more or less as extra instruments, and when their nature rebels — when they desperately assert their difference — Strauss gains an effect of strain and violence. Fundamental in Strauss was a certain simplicity — a simple sensualness and a taste for horseplay. But with this went a great astuteness which told him that in the 20th century such elementary things must be brought up to date. He did so with gusto, shouting from the housetops about necrophily (*Salomé*), birth control (*Die Frau ohne Schatten*), and one of Freud's complexes (*Elektra*), subjects not previously discussed in the opera house. A bold, extravagant man! But after all we are not persuaded that there is any real vice in him. Only, with all his talent, his art seems somewhat factitious. We are reminded of Wilhelm II, a monarch blameless in private life, who at one time favoured a larger licentiousness in the night-life of Berlin, to bring his capital abreast of the most advanced civilization.

Straussian opera employs a highly coloured and eloquent orchestra, which is even more ready and profuse than Wagner's with explanations, so that the author's words are frequently made unnecessary and at the same time obliterated. *Der Rosenkavalier* is Strauss's *Meistersinger.* It is an elaborate and sumptuous music-picture of Maria Theresa's Vienna as the other was of Sachs's Nuremberg. In Hugo von Hofsmannthal Strauss found as good a librettist as Wagner had found in himself. The opera is hugely long and heavy; the personages are weighed down by Strauss's symphonic style (which he had transferred to opera from his concert-room practice), like Velázquez's infantas in their brocades. It remains a masterpiece, the best of the many of its time written for orchestra with vocal obbligati. For that matter, there are all-important pages towards the end of each one of the three acts where the terrible garrulousness of Strauss's orchestra is in abeyance and the voices on the stage can express themselves at an almost natural-seeming level. If old Vienna was not like this, we say (as before of old Nuremberg), then it should have been. Wagner sang of love; Strauss sings voluptuousness, the Marschallin's noble voluptuousness, the Baron's base and Octavian's precocious voluptuousness, in a society given to the most formal of fine manners and to savage horse-play, a society "rotten ere it be half ripe," like Rosalind's medlar.

* * * *

The most interesting of the minor schools of opera has been the Russian. But a word is also due to the Czechs, Smetana (1824-1884) and Dvořák (1841-1904). Each composed both comic and imposing legendary or historical operas deriving from Czech lore, which have enjoyed lasting appreciation at Prague, thanks to the favourable tide of nationalist feeling. *The Bartered Bride* (1866) and *The Kiss* (1876) were Smetana's masterpieces in his lighter vein; *Libuša* (1881) was less a drama than a solemn patriotic pageant. Dvořák's operas have not been successful outside Bohemia.

Russian opera was started on its interesting career by Glinka (1804-1857), a career which, at least to all appearances, ended with Rimsky-Korsakov (1844-1908). The outstanding works were: Glinka's *A life for the Tsar* and *Russlan and Ludmila;* Dargomizhsky's *Russalka* (1850) and *The Stone Guest* (posthumously performed, 1872); Mussorgsky's *Boris Godunov* (1874) and *Khovanstchina* (composed 1872-1880, unfinished, edited by Rimsky-Korsakov); Borodin's *Prince Igor* (unfinished, edited by Rimsky-Korsakov and Glazunov, 1889); and Rimsky-Korsakov's *Maid of Pskov* (1873), *Snow Maiden* (1882), *Sadko* (1897), *Tsar Saltan* (1900), *Golden Cock* (1910). The fifth of these was the culminating masterpiece. Russian opera before *Boris Godunov* was a preparation and afterwards came nothing of a comparable character or vitality. Glinka gave a lead to Russian musicians by his non-Germanic use of bright, unmixed colour. National instinct preserved Russian independence from Wagnerian chiaroscuro and eloquence. *The Stone Guest* (a Don Juan opera) was an attempt, quite in the spirit of the authors of the *stile rappresentativo,* to use music purely as a reinforcement of words. The result, as usual, was rather bleak; but Dargomizhsky inspired Mussorgsky.

Like *The Stone Guest, Boris* was a setting of a drama by Pushkin. It was composed in 1868-

1870; was performed at St. Petersburg in 1874; was neglected till 1889 (Moscow); then in 1896 was drastically revised by Rimsky-Korsakov.* "It is," said Debussy of Mussorgsky's music, "like the art of some curious barbarian whose sheer force of feeling opens to him, step by step, the way to music." The constituents of this music are: Russian folk-song (curiously harmonized), other vocal phrases immediately derived from speech (so that when Shaliapin sang *Boris* his singing seemed hardly less natural than speaking), and instrumental figures suggestive of the actors' gestures and characters. It is remarkable, and a proof of the musician's genius, that out of constituents so scrappy he sustained a consistent style; the style of *Boris* never fails — except in the Polish scene, where Mussorgsky was quite at a loss. Evidently it was not a music that could stand on its own feet. It needed a strong subject; it found a magnificent one in *Boris.* In truth, this Boris remains Pushkin's, just as *Pelléas* remains Maeterlinck's. Mussorgsky's music does not of itself expound the drama; even if it had had the strength, it was not called upon to do so. The drama is gripping; Mussorgsky's music preserves and

* Mussorgsky own *Boris* is accessible in the Oxford University Press's edition (1928).

enhances it — a German might have drowned
it in a symphonic flood. Yes, while the *Ring*
was still unfinished there came this new reform
from an untaught Muscovite — a way of pre-
serving personal drama in opera. The tragedy
of *Boris* — a tragedy of almost Shakespearian
truth and intensity — was too personal to be
generalized and dissipated in a musical com-
mentary. The conscience-stricken emperor is no
abstraction, but a living, individual man, as
vivid as Macbeth; that is the interest of the
piece, the high, sharp definition of Boris against
the grey sea of the feckless and innominate Russian multitude. Wotan and the rest are all en-
shrouded, as it were, in music. Their utterances
are sublime but confused, like a preacher's in an
echoing Gothic nave. But in the remote and
featureless wilds of Russia some acute personal
utterance is all-important; and it is our luck that
on that background Mussorgsky gave to the
singers in the foreground actors' parts, and to
the chief of them the part that the greatest actor
of the early 20th century found to be his best.
It would be otiose to compare the two musicians
as such. But there is a moral in that, at the
moment when Wagner was about to inundate
the West, the Russian composer, having a purpose of his own, found a way of his own to

effect it. The character and doom of Boris are
not matched by any of the numerous but weaker
interests of *Khovanstchina*. Of Rimsky-Korsakov's operas the satiric and fanciful *Golden
Cock* is perhaps the most attractive. The composer's strong point was a clear-cut national
style, an almost peasant-like art. His operas are
fairy-tales, the music is like the illustrations to
a child's book, cheerful, unpretentious and
mildly racy.

Opera in England, meanwhile, from Handel
to Strauss was principally an imported summer
luxury. But not entirely. A species of operetta —
the ballad opera — flourished in the 18th century. An early example, Gay's brilliant *Beggar's
Opera* (1728), the music of which was a cento
arranged by Pepusch, was satirical. The ballad
opera soon inclined towards light sentimentality. But again in the 19th century the most
vital form of English opera was parody, represented by Sullivan's (1842-1900) long series of
Savoy operettas, which captivated the English-
speaking world with their humorous charm. An
innumerable public has *The Mikado* by heart,
while it knows Sullivan's serious opera *Ivanhoe*
(1891) only by name.* Similarly Arne's ballad

* *Ivanhoe* enjoyed the greatest immediate succes of
any serious opera. With a double company it ran for

opera *Love in a Village* of 1762 is familiar to many who have never even heard of his *opera seria* of the same year, *Artaxerses.* The moral often drawn is that a national or racial disability stands between us and achievement in the higher forms of the lyric stage.

The much more likely explanation of the shortcomings in the tale of English opera is economic. It is to be found in the lack here of any but irregular and uncertain support, while abroad opera was a fixed charge upon monarch or state. Music as modern Europe knows it depends upon settled conditions and a permanent establishment to a degree that the English have never been willing to face. It is not that interest in opera has been wanting. For two centuries aristocratic subscribers and daring impresarios between them kept London well informed — the masterpieces of Continental opera and the best exponents were seldom long in finding their way hither — while in the country people always had a welcome for the makeshift opera of travelling companies. Sometimes these last have, although on the same footing economically as any commercial entertainment, risen for a period to a level of performance below that

160 nights. Composed in 1890, it belonged rather to the European style of 40 years before.

of only the greatest European theatres. Such were the Carl Rosa company (founded 1875) in its early days, the Denhof company (1910-12) and the Beecham company (a continuation of Denhof's, which itself was continued from 1922 under the name British National Opera Company).

Their hold on life was too uncertain for adequate encouragement to a school of composition. English operas have mostly been written either with a merely imaginary stage in mind, or too much under the pressure of provincial restrictions. Remarkable in the circumstances is the number of them that have come to birth. The "little renascence" of English music early in Victoria's reign was represented in opera by Barnett, Balfe (whose *Siege of Rochelle* ran for three months at Drury Lane, and whose *Bohemian Girl* enjoyed world-wide success), Loder, Wallace and Macfarren. The last quarter of the 19th century saw a growth of English music from deeper roots. Parry, Mackenzie and Elgar wrote no operas, but Stanford (1852-1924) produced several, beginning with *The Veiled Prophet* of 1881, and including *Much Ado about Nothing* (Covent Garden, 1901).

Ethel Smyth aimed at the continental stage with *Der Wald* (Dresden and Covent Garden

1902) and her ambitious and effective *Wreckers* (Leipzig 1906, London 1909). *The Boatswain's Mate* (1916) was nearly a success; only the music expanded beyond the interest of the action.* Holbrooke, a Wagnerian disciple, wrote a trilogy of a gloom that makes Erda and the Norns seem comparatively jolly. Boughton's *Immortal Hour* (1914) was a musical echo, pretty but belated, of the romantical Burne-Jonesiana fashionable a generation before.

Characteristic and delightful music went to the making of Vaughan Williams's *Hugh the Drover* (1924) and *Sir John in Love* (1929), and Holst's *Savitri* (1916) and *The Perfect Fool* (1923), but into none of these works has the composer put his whole self — not one of them represents quite the centre of the man. More nearly entire is the Delius of *A Village Romeo and Juliet* (Berlin, 1907, London, 1910). This is a work not less distinct and not less poetic than Debussy's opera, from which, however, it differs radically. The focus of interest in *Pélleas et Mélisande* lies in the utterances of the characters, subdued though they are; Delius's orchestra

*"An opera is a superposition of one drama upon another; and the difficulty of its construction is the difficulty of making the two dramas, the musical and the non-musical, coincide." (E. J. Dent.)

is, German-fashion, the vehicle of his expression
and poetry, and the actors are left to do what
they can with spatchcocked vocal parts.

*   *   *   *

In the second decade of the 20th century the
long decline of the language of classical music
came to a crisis, and this coincided with the
agitation and incoherence in Europe consequent
upon the sufferings and destruction of the 1914
war. It is a question whether this coincidence
was accidental or part of a larger phenomenon
recognized in Germany as "der Untergang des
Abendlandes". The musical development was
unfavourable to vocal music; desperate experi-
ments were tried in the field of opera, but the
period was principally distinguished by a revival
of spectacular dancing at the expense of lyric
drama. Stravinsky's operas were insignificant,
but his ballet *Petrushka* (1912) a masterpiece.
In England Vaughan Williams's *Job* (1931)
was a work more profound and vital than his
charming operas.

Igor Stravinsky (b. 1882) was a Parisianized
Russian. Another representative figure was
Arnold Schoenberg (b. 1874), a Viennese Jew.
Both, as elderly men, became Americanized.

Their ways were far separated, but each developed a style hostile to vocal expression — Stravinsky, one of primitive modality violently coloured by dissonance, and Schoenberg an ultra-chromaticism from which every diatonic element was excluded. Schoenberg demanded from the voice a kind of feline wailing.

Stravinsky's stiff vocal writing, e.g. in the comic opera *Mavra* (1922) and the so-called opera-oratorio *Oedipus Rex* (1927), makes for an effect of parody. Independent of both these masters was Paul Hindemith (b. 1895), who applied to the stage the busy, mechanical style that had recommended his clever instrumental music to a disillusioned generation. When he came to a subject requiring a certain degree of warmth, *Mathis der Maler* (1934), his cold-bloodedness was seen to be a deficiency, not merely assumed.

Alban Berg (1885-1935), the most considerable of Schoenberg's pupils, composed *Wozzeck* (produced Berlin, 1925), the subject of which is a psychopath, and left unfinished *Lulu* (produced Zürich, 1937), whose subject is a prostitute — the period having been one in which respectability was at a discount. While representative of a self-pitying generation much given to commiserating with life's misfits — waiters who hated waiting and sailors who were afraid of going to sea — *Wozzeck,* the drama of a subnormal type who finds himself in the army without the least qualification for the soldier's life, rose above most of that generation's achievements by reason of Berg's rare art and rare sensibility. His feeling was genuine, his style abstruse but unmistakably fine. The score of *Wozzeck* speaks wonderfully for Viennese music in the last stage of its decadence. Less deeply eccentric but, all the same, odd enough was Darius Milhaud's *Christophe Colomb* (composed 1928, produced Berlin, 1930), which was an elaborate attempt to transform the history of 1492 into Christian myth, with the aid of varied paraphernalia, including the cinema.

In England ripples from such currents were felt years later in Benjamin Britten's operas, *Peter Grimes* (Sadler's Wells, 1945) and *The Rape of Lucretia* (Glyndebourne, 1946). The sinister protagonist of the former is another of the psychopaths dear to the Germany of 20 years before; the latter piece, deriving from a French play, endeavours to find significance where Shakespeare himself could find none, by comparing Lucretia with the Founder of Christianity. The music of these works revealed an extraordinary talent, agile and inventive, with no